Memories of Hainault

Local Stories
By Local People

© Hainault Community Centre Writers Group

ISBN 0-9552894-0-8

Published by Hainault Writers 2006

Hainault Writers
Hainault Forest Community Centre,
100b Manford Way,
Chigwell,
Essex.
ᛐ IG7 4DF

Printed and bound in Great Britain by
Trade Print Europe
72 New Bond Street
London W1S 1RR
www.printeurope.co.uk

Contents

Contents

INTRODUCTION
The Start

Extract from
ILFORD & REDBRIDGE WEEKLY POST
Friday 7th. November 2003

A writers group are looking for inspiration from residents who have a fond memory or an interesting tale to tell about Hainault. Redbridge Council have just given Hainault Writers Group £2.500 to produce an anthology of stories about the area, and members are now looking to track down people who can contribute to the book. Secretary of the group Beryl Bridger said: "There are a lot of elderly people living in the area who have many stories which need to be historically put down. Some of these people are getting very old and if we don't take these stories down now they could be lost forever.

"We are looking for as many people as possible to contribute to the book. It really is going to be a trip down memory lane as far back as we can. One of our writers is 86 years old & he has spent the biggest part of his life in Hainault and remembers so much.

Mrs Bridger is also keen to get young people involved and she hopes Hainault Forest High school pupils will take part in the project. She said: "We are looking to speak to people of all ages as it would be nice to bring the book right up to date Anyone interested in contributing to the book should contact the Hainault Community Centre on 020 8500 4311

After two and a half years of endeavour we are pleased to present our book and hope that you Dear Reader find it all worthwhile

The Hainault Writers Group

ACKNOWLEDGMENTS

We thank Redbridge Council, Area 3
And Councillor Mrs Joyce Ryan for their
support and sponsorship without which
this book could not have been published.

Mick Willis MBE and Staff of
The Hainault Community Centre
For their support over the years

Photographs reproduced from
Volumes 1, 2 and 4 of
'Ilford Old and New'
By kind permission of Mr B. Piggott.

Drawings reproduced from watercolours
by A. Middleton-Blaney
and J. Britton.

Book cover front & back designed and
painted by our member Ivy Brown

Excerpts from Mr. W. Coles book
50 years of Hainault Church's

All who submitted their stories and photographs

Greene King Brewery for their generous donation

Alan & Kathy Hemmings for their assistance in
preparing our manuscript for printing

A HAIKU 4 HAINAULT

COMMUNITY LED

HAINAULT'S TOWN SPIRIT IS FED

BY KEEPING AHEAD

Foreword

**Life / Memories are Ephemeral.
But the Written Word Endures**

People generally may be called 'Ordinary People' but many of them have extra-ordinary stories of things they have experienced in their lifetimes, but they never speak of them as they think they are nothing extra-ordinary and very rarely do they write them down and eventually they are lost forever and we are all the poorer because history as they experienced it will never be known.

As a writing group we have endeavoured to try to obtain access to local residents who have a story as to how Hainault and it's environs were before and even after the Estate was built. In this we have achieved a measure of success and are pleased with the the responses we have had to enable us to produce this book, but we are sure there are many more of you out there who have similar experiences in their memories, although no two people would have exactly the same story to tell.

We hope you will enjoy reading this book and will be a little more aware of the changes that have taken place in this area in our lifetimes.

Origin Of The Name Hainault And Events
By Jack Farmer

Hainault And Hog Hill House

The Saxon name of Henholt becomes Hainault. It is translated into the name of a part of Belgium from which an English Queen came.

1600's. In the early 1600's, Waltham Forest extended from Bow Bridge, Stratford to the Bridge at Abridge and included Ilford. It later became commonly known as Hainault Forest.

1646. It has been recorded that, around 1646, there was a Chapel Hainault Lodge possibly on the site of Hog Hill House. The old house was rebuilt in 1725 when it was described as a 'large brick house'.

1794. At the Maypole, Barkingside, on the 12th June 1794 there was a sale by auction, of lops and tops taken off 372 Oak trees prepared for His Majesty's Navy. The lops and tops were lying near Hog Hill House in Hainault Forest.

1848. Hainault Forest School, opened in May 1848, has 76 children. The buildings are adapted for 102 children. The School was built by donations and annual subscriptions.

1852. In the Illustrated London News of 1852 there is a wood engraving of Hog Hill House and it is possibly the only pictorial record of the old house.

1853. The Royal approval of the deforestation was reported in 1853 and the clearance of large areas began. This led to extensive building in the East of London helped by the development of the railways.

Hainault House was built on the site of Hog Hill House after the forest was cut down. It was a large substantial country house. When it was built there was open country on all sides. It was a crown lease house and the last private person to live there was Colonel Gibbons (in the 1930's), a Deputy Lieutenant of Essex. It later became an annexe for Oldchurch Hospital and was demolished in 1971. It is now a wildlife reserve.

Back to Hainault Forest, the L.C.C. paid half of £21,380 required by the Crown, the rest was paid by E.C.C., West Ham, Leyton, Wanstead and Ilford. The forest, covering 1018 acres, was the largest open space maintained by the L.C.C. and remains a treasured recreational park.

Another Version Of The Origin
By Arthur Salton

There are a number of theories as to where the name Hainault originated.
From Hainault in Germany.
Or as a compliment to Phillipa of Hainault the Consort of Edward the 3rd.
From the Anglo-Saxon Hean meaning poor, of little value (character of the land) hen and holt a Wood.
Another version is, it comes from Hayn (a clear enclosed space) and holt a wood, but then another say's it derives from 'Higna' and 'Holt' meaning the Wood of the Community, the Community then, being Barking Abbey to which it belonged.
Finally what is said to be the true derivative is the Anglo-Saxon Hean holt. The High Wood.
The name however first appeared in 1221 and was recorded as 'Hyneholt. The area was heavily wooded by what was then an extensive 'Hainault Forest', but when the enclosures act was passed in 1851, Land Owners and Land Grabbers claimed land and as a result deforestation was carried out. Deer were removed and the cutting of timber began and it was estimated that 10,000 trees, Oak, Beech, Hornbeam and others were cut down.
The legendary 'Fairlop Oak' symbolises Hainault, its fame spreading far and wide due to the efforts of Daniel Day, a Wapping Pump manufacturer who started what became the 'Fairlop Fair' that took place once a year beneath the branches of the great Oak.
This fabulous tree was said to be several hundred years old, its girth sixteen feet and its branches extended three hundred feet in circumference and the shadow cast by its branches covered an acre of ground or more. It became so decayed and hollow, that when a fire was lit inside it, it weakened it so much that it was blown down in 1820. Part of the timber from the tree was used by a builder to make a Pulpit and a Reading Desk for Saint Pancras Church Euston Road in London.
In 1922, another tree was planted at Fairlop Waters where the original was said to have stood.
In 1952, 60,000 East Londoners were moved to the new housing Estate in Hainault and other areas.

PEOPLE WHO HELPED PUT HAINAULT AND ITS SURROUNDING AREAS ON THE MAP

On the 5th December 1952, Albert Gunter was driving a number 78 bus and approached Tower Bridge when the road started to rise and opened up in front of him. He managed to stop the bus with the front wheels over the edge of the Bridge Road with the long drop into the River staring him in the face. For his prompt action in saving the bus and its passengers, he was awarded the princely sum of £10.00.

Alma Cogan a most popular singer of her time lived in Manor Road, Chigwell.

Dennis D'Ell the singer in the group 'Honeycombs' with a number one in the charts in 1960 'Have I the right'.

Bobby Moore, Professional Footballer, Captain of the England team that won the World Cup in 1966. Bobby's baby son was christened in the Church of the Immaculate Assumption in Manford Way.

Jimmy Greaves, Professional Footballer, played for England and was in the team with Bobby in 1966. Jimmy was also well known for his appearances on television for his comments on the football scene.

Tina Charles, the singer who had a number one in the charts in 1974 with 'I Love to Love'.

Colin Reitz, Top Steeple Chaser, who won the 3000 metres in the 1986 Olympics.

Sally Gunnel, Athlete, Olympic Gold Medal winner in 1996.

Ronnie O'Sullivan, World Snooker Champion in 1999.

Bob Crow, Leader of the R.M.T. Union went to Kingswood School in Hainault.

Hainault Forest Community Centre, established when the new Estate was built just after World War Two and has played an active role in providing many different activities to the Community as a whole, including a well run Bar and over the years has gone from strength to strength.

A FORMAL HISTORY OF HOW THE ASSOCIATION HAS DEVELOPED OVER THE PAST 18 YEARS
June 2004

Since 1986 there has been a specific target regarding the facilities and activities to be made available to users. There were two main issues that needed to be addressed before the action plan could be instigated.

1. ANNEXE BUILDING

This area needed major refurbishment work if it was to continue to play a part in the Association's future. Rooms were dilapidated and the flat roof was continually in need of repair to alleviate water leakage.

2. MAIN BUILDING

This consisted of a small bar area, main hall with a badminton court and an office area. It was apparent that major refurbishment was required to encourage residents to use our facilities and to add other rooms to increase activities for such use.

The activities within the Annexe building in 1986, consisted of Citizens Advice Bureau, 12 child Nursery facility, Dog Training and Karate.

It was imperative that a pitched roof was erected to eradicate future leaks. This was carried out by London Borough of Redbridge in accordance with their responsibilities as Landlords and terms of our lease.

The Citizens Advice Bureau at that time occupied two small offices and a waiting area and due to their increase in users, it was agreed to transfer them into what was our childcare facility. This then enabled us to facilitate the Day Nursery within the main annexe area which was now free of water leakage. Investment was required to use the whole area as a Day Nursery for 2-5 year olds. At this time, it did not fall within the Boroughs remit to fund pre-school education.

It was apparent to our management committee, however, that there was a definite need for both parents of a family to return to work and that our role as a Community Association should be to provide a low cost affordable facility for local parents.

12

Funding was obtained from private trust grant foundations and the Association itself.
Numbers of placements were increased gradually from 12 to 39 for 2-5 year olds .
In 1999 we realised the need for mums to return to work earlier following maternity leave.
We obtained registration for a 7 place (3mths. - 2 years) area to assist parents and this proved very popular, once again, this was funded by the Association.

Summary
The position within the annexe building was now a purpose built CAB and a much improved OFSTED registered childcare facility.

In 2001 the Association was approached by Redbridge Children's Information Service to ascertain the possibility of sharing the CAB facility (as the CAB only used it 2 days a week). This was due to the premises currently used by CIS being far from adequate.

Lengthy discussions ensued and it was finally agreed satisfactorily with all parties concerned that the CIS occupy all the area in question with the CAB moving to our main building.

Accordingly a sub-lease was drawn up by local services and the Association received £100 per week rent which includes all heating, lighting and cleaning costs.

Due to the need for additional childcare places our Nursery was seen as an ideal facility to be included within the Redbridge Neighbourhood Nursery Initiative .

Funding was available from New Opportunities Fund, Redbridge Primary Care Trust, Sure Start and the Standards Fund.
Obviously we needed to meet certain criteria and following numerous meetings we were successful with our application.

This has enabled our childcare placements to be increased from 39 to 70, 27 of which are children aged 3 months - 2 years. This project was formally opened in the presence of The Mayor, Vanessa Cole and Linda Perham, M.P. on the 14th. February 2004.

Main Building

In 1990 it was decided that if the Association was to move forward it needed to generate additional income.

Major refurbishment took place within the Bar area which doubled it's size and offered a comfortable welcoming facility for users.

It was funded by a £100,000 unsecured Brewery loan from Greene King which has since been repaid.

This project proved to be successful and with the additional sales it became inevitable that a larger beer cellar would be necessary.

An additional sum of £15,000 was funded by the Association.

Having completed the Bar improvements it was decided to look at the Main Hall. Initially a suspended ceiling and air duct system were installed at a cost of £10,000 met by the Association. This gave the area a warmer effect but the flooring had passed it's sell-by date. In partnership with our landlords (LBR) a new floor was laid at a cost of £10,000. It became apparent to our landlords, Education Services, that our Management Committee had a definite vision for the Centre's future. To enable us to fulfil our aims and objectives the Council funded the erection of three rooms to facilitate additional activities.

These rooms are now in constant use, not only generating additional income but also providing ideal meeting areas for organisations such as Hainault neighbourhood Wardens, local Police Working Party and the Children's Information Service. We do not charge the first two bodies any rent as we see their work as an important service to the community. The local Citizens Advice Bureau also now uses part of the area and a nominal rent only is charged because of their valued service.

The Association Development Plans have always stated that new activities must be sought to ensure we 'keep up with the times'.

It is to this end we applied for funding and planning for a UK Online Computer Suite.

You will be aware that the above were successful and the suite was formally opened in August 2002. The use and success has exceeded our expectations.

It provides free access to users who would otherwise have no contact with information technology and has given people a new interest in their lives, especially senior citizens.

This activity is run in partnership with Redbridge Institute of Adult Education (RIAE), who provide the tutors for courses.
The administration, budgeting and allocation of users is dealt with by the Associations staff.
We must thank Area 3 Committee for their valued financial support since the inception of this project.

We have a three year contract with the funding body (Government Office for London, GOL) to provide the current service which expires in August 2005. We shall be making arrangements with RIAE as to the facilities future use following this date.

The additional workload on the administrative staff, bearing in mind the extra staff and activities now within the Association, has led to the current office being far from adequate to cope with these demands.

It is with this end that we have applied for planning permission to have a new office built with the present area being used as an extension of the Bar area.
Once planning has been accepted we will put the proposed works out to tender to obtain definite prices for funding applications.

If this project is successful I think it would be fair to say that the Association has more than fulfilled it's constitutional aims and objectives over the past 18 years.

This does not mean that we can relax for the future and the Management Committee, together with the salaried staff, must always look for ways of improving our standards.

We are in the early stages of acquiring an 'Investors in People' accreditation through Business Link for Essex. If we are successful it will provide us with the satisfaction that our business is being run in

I accordance with recognised standards

All members must be aware that this is their Association and it is only successful because of individuals efforts

It is imperative that 'new faces' come to both the Social Club and Association's Management Committees.
It is sometimes a thankless task but much satisfaction can be gained when you know your efforts are rewarding many people.

This year Mick Willis, Centre Organiser, was awarded the MBE for his services to the community of Hainault.

Mick's Story
By Mick Willis MBE

I have lived in Hainault since 1971 when I moved from Barking. I moved into Dryden Close which was a very tightly knit community, much like the 'old days' when neighbours spoke to each other and were always there when someone was in need.

I was fortunate to live next door to George & Kay Duffree . George always made himself available, especially if you had a problem with your car or needed some D.I.Y. tips.

Our community in Dryden Close gradually began to disperse when people had the opportunity to purchase their small flats and saw this as an ideal opportunity to get their foot on the property ladder and move to larger abodes.

Sad, but that's what today's money orientated world has created, more individual wealth but poorer social inclusion.

I became a member of the HFCA in 1980 and had no idea at that time that much of my future would be dedicated to the Centre.

It was early in 1986 that the Association was not very well supported by active Committee members and I was approached to ascertain whether I would be interested in supporting the cause. My initial reaction was that as I had no experience of Committee work I felt it outside my remit. Obviously, I was persuaded otherwise and have gained much pleasure in being part of a dedicated team in bringing the Association to the high esteem it is now held by the local authority.

I have compiled a brief history of the Centre over the past 20 years which I hope you will find interesting.

In 2003, I personally, was overwhelmed to be nominated for and received an MBE from Her Majesty the Queen. It was a surreal day for both my family and myself.

The Centre's popularity and success afforded a visit from Cherie Blair in April 2004, accompanied by Linda Perham, then MP for Ilford North. They visited all the area's of the Centre and were amazed at the wide variety of activities that took place

Organisations such as ours can only succeed on team effort and dedication. We work on a very tight budget and are totally dependent on income derived from our services.

Long may Hainault Forest Community Association continue to prosper!

Charabanc

Photograph by Jack Hall

All ready for the off, Members of The Hainault Community Centre
in Manford Way pose for the camera in 1950 alongside the 'Charabanc'
that will take them to somewhere on the South Coast

Hainault Forest Community Centre
I.T. Suite

Escape Tunnels in Chigwell
By Margot S Cooper

The old boys grammar school in Chigwell started life under the first Headmaster Samuel Harsnett (1561-1631). Still on the site stands the current Chigwell School which welcomes boys and girls with David Gibbs as the current Headmaster.

"Chigwell, my dear fellow, is the greatest place in the world"...so Charles Dickens wrote to his friend John Forster.

The properties that line either side of the road are rarely looked at as one speeds through in a motor car. If you are held up in traffic, have a look at the buildings. The cream painted Essex clapboard style cottages, the red brick of the school, the ancient stones of the church.

You have to see the Old Kings Head Public House as it almost hangs over the road. The Tudor look came in the 1930's and has stayed. A very young proprietor, L Stansall in 1936 took over the run down, dilapidated house which had been The Maypole in Dickens time.

Underneath were cellars and tunnels going towards Arnot Cottages, another towards the old vicarage, an escape route for the blue beard priest (house ghost) and another southwards towards a much rumoured monastery?

They were probably wine cellars, when unsealed the sherry butts disappeared overnight into the dust and a few torpedo shaped bottles were found, but empty. One inquisitive pupil Jimmy Ramsey along with Kelly (Paul Calthorp) and Kit Cuttle decided that there must be a tunnel to the Kings Head. A rumour being that at one stage a Headmaster Mr Edwards in 1810 had one pupil and doubled as publican.

The trio appeared to like digging and encouraged others to join them as they had already dug a Neolithic pit dwelling.

Jim, Kelly and Kit got up at 2 am daily in the summer term of 1954. They took the floor boards up in the cleaners cupboard went down six feet and then forward parallel to the building for about eight feet trying to get to the mysterious staircase.

Stopping work at about 5 am the soil and dirt was put into the flower beds. For quite a few weeks at the foundation level they made a hole taking out the bricks and shoring up the hole. They just missed out on reaching the staircase and discovered rubbish from the twenties just as the end of term came along.

More proper building work took place in 1978 when Big school was being renovated into a new library. Two more feet further and a chest was found full of books and deeds dating back to the 18th century as well as a fireplace 378 years old.

Go gently and slowly along the road, how many more tunnels are there?

Acknowledgements to Mrs Marion Delfgou the Chigwell School Archivist for supplying the letter from James B Ramsey and other material.

Mr Walter Coles Story

In 1940 a stick of bombs fell on Ilford Lane and his house and new home were destroyed and he moved to Newcastle Avenue in Hainault. On the 21st of September his first night there, the siren's sounded. Anti-Aircraft gun's opened up and a Parachute Land Mine fell on houses in Lime Grove and Chestnut Grove devastating the area.

His house in Newcastle Avenue was left without doors, windows or ceilings and half the roof was missing. Workmen came in and carried out emergency repairs, nailing up doors and putting roofing felt over windows. Ceilings, walls and floors were just left as they were and remained that way for the next five years.

An Air Raid Warden who lived in Lime Grove, on duty in New North Road, saw the mine descending. He could have taken shelter, but thinking only of warning his neighbours, he raced to their houses only to arrive at the same time as the mine exploded. It injured him so badly that he died a few hours later. For his unselfish act he was awarded a 'Gold Cross' for heroism, the first awarded to anyone in the Ilford area.

Walking home with his wife on a Saturday night along Fencepiece Road, Anti Aircraft guns blazed away at a landmine drifting down on a parachute and lit up by searchlights.It passed over their heads as they lay flat on their faces in someone's front garden. The mine landed, exploding on the 'Prince of Wales' Public House in Manor Road killing 80 people.

A sports pavilion behind Stoke Avenue was a meeting place for the Leysian Mission. Everything was rationed then and petrol more strictly so and one member at least would arrive driving a pony and trap. After meeting there on a few Sundays, they arrived one day to find all their belongings outside on the grass and workmen busy installing a metal press, drilling machines and lathes. The building had been commandeered for war work. At the time one of the members had a Drapers shop at 200 New North Road by Hainault Station.

In 1940 after the Battle of Britain most of the houses in Hainault were empty and up for let. Fairlop Aerodrome was a base for Spitfires and Hurricanes and fighter planes were taking off and landing day and night. To keep them in the air, a large contingent of Pilots, Air Crew, Mechanics and Women's Auxiliary Air Force were billeted in huts and buildings in Forest Road.

While the war was on, with the evacuation of women and children and men being drafted into the Forces, Hainault was deserted. It was a ghost town and it wasn't until after the war with Germany ending on the 8th May 1945 that people started to return.

To help the war effort as part of 'The Dig For Victory' campaign, all sports fields, football and rugby grounds were ploughed up to grow corn, making certain every space possible was used to produce food that otherwise had to be brought in by the Royal and Merchant Navy's who ran the gauntlet of getting through German U Boat packs that prowled the sea.

Mr Cole, who ran a garage on the corner of New North Road and Tunstall Avenue, found time to take over the running of the 'Boys Brigade' that had been restarted in 1942 and in 1943 he had orders to take the Hainault Brigade to Windsor. It was all shrouded in secrecy as they were to be reviewed by King George VI. The King inspected the ranks and everyone was surprised by his 'terribly tired and wrinkled face' that was a shock to all who saw him, but it was a proud moment for everyone involved.

In 1947, he started Hainault Football Club, the team was known as 'Hainault Sports'. The Senior Boy's team were the Ilford Youth Champion's for three years running.

He ran the garage for 16 years until it was demolished in the late 50's and a petrol station built in its place. The petrol station itself has now gone and has been replaced by a block of flats.

There was a plan to build another church in the Lowe and a plot of land was reserved for the building, but owing to the close proximity of St Paul's in Arrowsmith Road and the Assembly Church in Manford Way, it was decided not to and the land was developed into houses and flats, in what is now Lowe Close.

With acknowledgement to Mr W Cole's book '50 Years in the Hainault Churches'.

Hainault Of Yesteryear And Now

By A Salton 10.11.05.

Hainault and the surrounding area has changed so much in the last 200 years that it is surprising to see that so many place names are shown on a map published in 1777 and these names were no doubt around for many more years before that and it's lovely that they are still there to-day after all those years, although the spelling now may be different.

Hainault, Henhault as it was called then, is said to have originated from the Anglo-Saxon words Higna and Holt meaning 'The Wood Of The Community', Hainault Forest. This is said to be the true version of where the name came from, although there are other schools of thought as to its origins.

Trawling through the 1777 map, the forest then was about three and a half miles wide by two and half deep, covering the areas where pre-war houses and the post war Estate has been built.

It stretched from Woodford Bridge to Collier Row at its widest point and from Chigwell Row to Padnall Corner just below Marks Gate. The name Padnall still exists as the name of a road and a close.

Towards Collier Row in the forest, an open space encloses a building 'New Chapel Lodge' and above that well inside the forest is 'Hog Hill' and on it is shown 'Henhault Lodge'. Above that is 'Hog Hill Pond' that seems to have been where the reservoir is located.

The 'Fairlop Oak', the tree, is shown in the forest and its position on the map places it where Fairlop Waters is now. It was on a level with the 'Maypole' pub in Barkingside and another 'Maypole' pub also existed at the edge of Collier Row.

The 'Fairlop Oak', the tree, was the site for the annual Fair held for many years around and even inside its massive hollow trunk. The Fair started by Daniel Day in 1776 became notorious for riotous goings on until the authorities eventually banned it.

Where Collier Row is now was 'Collier Row Common', a green area about one and three quarter miles long and half a mile wide. Off Collier Row is 'Cheese Cross' which is now remembered as 'Chase Cross' Road.

'Marks Gate' a well-known spot was there then and is now the stopping place for the No 62 bus service. There were other gates nearby 'Rose Lane Gate' (we still have Rose Lane) 'Abury Gate' and

'Collier Row Gate'. All the Gates were there as turnpikes to collect tolls from anyone passing through.

'Fencepiece' wasn't a road then, it was a clearing in the forest near to Claybury and a brick kiln was located there.

Chigwell Row is well in evidence and a small clearing is named 'Bowles'. From other information it seems there was an association with Sir Francis Drake and one of the present cottages called 'The Bowls' still exists there and that is where he was said to have stayed. Going towards Lambourne End what is the 'Camelot' pub now was then called the 'Maypole'.

In the other direction the spot where 'Grange Hill' underground station now stands was covered by the forest and on the opposite side of the road that ran by, stood 'Grange Hill Farm'.

Further on was 'Tomswood', 'Mossford Green' is spelt as 'Mossfoot Green' and 'Abury' and 'Abury Hatch' have metamorphosed into 'Aldborough' and 'Aldborough Hatch'.

'Great Gubbings' has given rise to 'Gubbins Lane' and ' Gravel Lane' and 'Pudding Lane' were both in existence then as was 'Little London' which is still there off Gravel Lane.

There was a 'Great Geris' and a 'little Geris' still there as 'Little Gearies' and just outside Barkingside. Towards Chigwell was a 'Chigwell Hatch' and below 'Abury Gate' was a 'Abury Hatch' Hatch being old English for grating.

Chigwell had a 'Free School' and 'Rolls' near Chigwell was occupied by a William Harvey, 'Rolls became 'Rolls Park' and in later years was occupied by Elia Harvey who commanded H.M.S. Temeraire that fought in the battle of Trafalgar and was the subject of the famous painting by Turner The Fighting Temerair' and the story goes that the timber from Hainault Forest was used in the building of the Temeraire. The Oak Trees that grew in Hainault Forest were of the type most suitable for building the wooden ships of the Navy and at the end of the 1700's almost 500 Loads of timber from the Forest, One load of Oak Timber contained 50 cubic feet. It must have cleared a large expanse of the forest but it took 3000 loads to build one ship.

In later years the Forest went into decline as materials were removed, trees, large areas of turf, bushes and undergrowth were cut down, gravel and sand dug out of the ground and Deer poaching was at its height. Black mutton (Venison) available to everyone.

The Temeraire

www.abcgallery.com

The launching of the Temeraire
at Chatham, on September 11, 1798

27

What Happened to my Heaven
By John Bartholomew

I were born to Fiddlers Hamlet, yonder by way begotten in a frenzy, in a field of Hainault Hay. My father was a wanderer who walked by now and then, I was told he he took one look at me and was never seen again

My mother was a big buxom wench all of eighteen stone, me poor little bugger was nought but skin and bone. I lived a life of freedom in and out those fields so green, even more exciting were the bits of forest in between.

Proud Oaks, Silver Birch and twisted Hornbeams flourished there, I became an expert catching both the Rabbit and the Hare. Badgers lived on the hill we called Brocket Way, intriguing the long Rabbit mound named Burrow Road today.

The Arrowsmith fashioned my first bow and taught me how to shoot, the very first victim of the fletcher was a Bald Faced Coot. I never killed for pleasure, no matter what I shot, we were poor enough and hungry much more often than not.

Farmer Manford had three fields verging on Romford Road. One he fattened young Bullocks in, the other two he sowed. One day all his stock escaped, it was nearly a total loss servicing every Cow in sight with a new breed called Manford Cross.

So my growing years went by and I were happy as could be, never dreaming what the future held in store for me, I were trapped I were, silly me, like a rabbit in a snare no matter were I went, I only had to turn my head and she were there.

She kept on and on, her grinning face fair got me in a muddle, I rolled her in that Hainault Hay , just a tickle and a cuddle, different altogether had I done her in clover.

They all called to harass my old mum, saying we should wed, all her father got for his pains was a pisspot over his head, they went away swearing and threatening to get even, I had a right old punch up with her older brother Stephen.

Things got very hot for me just as war broke out, for Stephen had been murdered without a shadow of doubt, he had been shot with a rifle bullet right in the back of the head and I was the very first suspect the minute they found him dead.

They found the rifle the very next day, finger prints wiped clean. For the life of me I could not remember where on earth I'd been, I knew I had been to a party and got drunk but nothing further, in no time at all I was indited for murder.

The old lady took it very hard, she nearly went insane.
I had reason enough and time enough, the evidence was plain.
In number one court at the Old Bailey, police evidence seemed to falter after some debate, they dropped the charge to manslaughter.

I will never forget that terrible day waiting for the finding, when they found me guilty, inside it was like a coil unwinding . I was sentenced to fifteen years, no chance of leniency.
No one will ever know what those long years did to me.

They let me out a month ago, with a suit and seventy pounds. I have never got over the shock, since I've done the rounds, my home has gone, I'm on my own, relatives are all dead, where our caravan had rested they have built The Alfred's Head.

My fields are all little boxes, full of people, dogs and cats, smelly cars and concrete roads interspersed with bloody flats, I have lived out here in Hainault since I was barely seven.
Why, oh why, did this have to happen to my idea of Heaven.

People have to live somewhere, I am quite aware of their pains, the only reason they took my fields was because of bloody trains.
There is a sequel to all this, wry jokes come no bigger, before my old lady died, she said,
It was her who pulled the trigger!!!

Betty's Story.
'Demolished' or Summer Suns are growing

Be warned I am having trouble separating the factual from the lyrical -so here goes- When I was born in Buckhurst Hill Hospital in 1926, Chigwell Row was a charming small village, separated from Hainault by fields and woodland later engulfed Hainault Estate.

We lived in 'Olive House', sadly demolished along with other interesting dwellings in Romford Road to make way for the estate - rumoured to be filled with an alien race of 'East Enders!

The busy two lane road now replaces the dusty, rural road to Romford. Traversed by my Grandfather in his horse and cart. The weeping Ash that held my swing and four trees at our front gate are what remains.

I happily recall romping and playing hide and seek in the hay sheds, the exciting visit of the Italian Hokey Pokey Man in his gaudy cart and picking blackberries in 'Butchers Wood', which bordered our garden.

Trotting across the forest beside my father to 'Foxburrows Farm' carrying a metal-lidded jug, which was dipped into Mr Taskers enormous milk churn, the churn and I being of similar size.

Trudging up the hill past the church to visit Miss Reads shop, returning clutching a paint box containing gold and silver paints.

I walked to the village school and still recall seeing the spiders webs hanging from the Hawthorn hedgerows glistening with raindrops. Sometimes we took a shortcut through the forest where in spring, Violets nestled on mossy banks, Cadmium Yellow King Cups, Bluebells and Lord and Ladies flowered.

Harebells and delicately pink Dog Roses in the Rec. magically appeared as summer approached. In the field adjacent to Carole's house (in Chigwell Row) Buttercups rioted; it was an exhilarating experience to run through them following in the childhood footsteps of my mother and her siblings.

Naturally there were dismal days, getting soaked to the skin and disgusting smells in the damp school cloakroom. So in a lyrical mood I continue. There truly was Maypole Dancing in the Rec. Fetes and cricket matches. George Harman who is remembered for his service to the church in the village hall, was a stalwart player.

Phil and George inherited the builders and undertakers from their father Frank. It operated from a building known as 'Row of Doves Nest' (behind the present Newsagent). I feel strongly that such a delightful name should be remembered. George papered my sitting room so perfectly; it is still in place, in good nick fifty years later.

Facing the Rec. in Manor Road was a Sunday school whose unusual doors are the front doors of the house, which replaced it. I have a love/hate relationship with Sunday school. I enjoyed the Christmas treats and coach outings to Southend, but otherwise did my best to hide and avoid singing 'Summer Suns are Glowing' when outside the glowing afternoon and the forest beckoned.

Near it is 'Hainault Hall' (Queen Anne. See Pevsner) which has been faithfully restored apart from an abundance of wrought iron. The family of Arthur Hughes, founder of Kelvin Hughes lived there. Mrs Hughes was Swedish and was considered eccentric because her children ran barefoot in spite of them being well heeled. Their son Gordon was a Spitfire Pilot and looped the loop over Chigwell Row to signal his safe return from a mission.

Manor Road was graced by several fine houses commissioned by rich London Merchants, some were more ancient. My Aunt lived in one 'The Grove', which was an Elizabethan House. We sometimes spent an atmospheric Christmas there. log fires and a huge fireplace heating the wood panelled rooms. There was nut walk which she loved.

'Foxhounds' previously an Inn, housed the Lewis family whose Grandmother was Elizabeth Garrett Anderson, the first woman Doctor. 'Frog Hall' where Mr Rigby lived is still there, he was a lynch pin of United Dairies and kindly lent his tennis court to our Youth Club.

Sir Francis Chichester lived awhile in the 18th century house behind the Chapel, which is also of that era. Before our present Church was built around the 1870's, local Christian villagers worshipped there.

'Socketts Cottages' facing the Rec, housed a 'Dame School' ruled over by a Miss Kitkat when my Great, Great Grandmother (Anne Hauce) attended there around the 1830's. One cottage is called 'School House'. George Shillibeer of Horse Bus fame, lived in 'Shillibeer Lane'. Maybe it could be uglified into 'Routemaster', another vehicle on the way out.

'Barrington Lodge (demolished) in the Rec was a former hunting lodge, Mrs Bixby a charismatic Artist lived there. 'The Bowls' (demolished) by Vicarage Lane. Legend has it that Sir Francis Drake was entertained there.

'Whitehall' in the direction of Lambourne End was demolished (I feel this memoir should be called demolished) and the present Whitehall Close stands on its grounds. The children of the Doctor who lived there owned a miniature railway running round the gardens perimeter and I greatly envied them as I peered through a hole in the fence. P D James was related to Dr Watts and lived there during the War years.

The most important building in my eyes was the sweet shop, now the newsagents which adjoined 'Whitehall's' grounds. Two delightful spinsters who had stepped out of 'Cranford' were its owners, the Misses Read and their shy bachelor Brother. I believe their gravestones are in the Chapel Churchyard.

I now live in the nearby weather boarded cottages (1878). I have heard that the timber used to construct them came from dismantled barns built at Hainault that were used to store grain for the expected invasion and siege of Napolean..

My family has inhabited this cottage since the early 1900's, as my Uncle ran the Hansom Cabs to Grange Hill and stabled his horses in the roomy area at the back of the house (where I am now writing). My Cousin Eddy Green, his Son, continued with the Village Taxi until his death about thirty years ago.

Jack Shepherd, an eccentric Greengrocer, traded in the area of Raymond Walk. Fruit and veg were sold in the yard behind his house. A large bell hanging from a coil rang loudly as you pushed the gate. Stepping round the pigs and hens, his elderly Mother served you. She was even in old age delicately pretty, usually wearing a cloth cap and sacking apron.

Her speech was impeccable and the story was 'she married beneath her'. Jack grazed horses in the field which was opposite the Guide Camp and I used to climb over the gate into the field - I had a irresistible urge to pick the bulrushes and water lilies growing in the pond, usually unsuccessfully.

I was delighted to discover Jack's memorial seat in the Forest, placed beside the pond called Ship or Sheep Waters amongst the woodland between the common and the 'Retreat' entrance.

Nearer to the common was the forge of Mr Albert Spain, village Blacksmith and keen Chapel man. A mighty man in all ways. Dawdling home from school, we would stop and peer into his mysterious fiery world unable to understand how the patient horses coped with their ordeal.

My Father owned the nearby Louvre Works. He had invented and patented the indoor Louvre, or plaster air vent, and was doing fine until World War Two put paid to building and his business - after the War the patent had expired.

My Dad was not famous or eccentric, but he was a 'Great' human being. Born in 1878 in Sydenham, he was at first a 'foreigner' usually known as Jane (Lizzie) Green's husband, at least during their early years together.

During the War he was an Air Raid Warden based in a shelter in the Rec. I used to cycle there with his cooked dinner insecurely in a knotted tea towel, the gravy spilling as I bumped along the uneven pavement. Bombs and landmines were dropped in the area (a time bomb fell just about where I was writing this in my Summer House).

The 'Prince of Wales' Pub received a direct hit killing two villagers. My friends Brother Peter Threader was killed in his teens having found an unexploded bomb.

The Threaders lived at Millers Farm in Millers Lane in charge of Miss Winnie Savills foxhounds. The farmyard was always swarming with lively hounds, the hunting term 'Hullabaloo' describes it perfectly.

Miss Winnie lived at 'Sheepcotes' (still there) on the way to Lambourne End. She was a keen Hunts Woman and point to pointer. I was a close friend of her Gardener and Chauffeur, George King - so heard amusing tales of her activities.

My Grandfather worked for Sir Phillip Savill, Miss Winnies Father. Sir Phillip owned 'Old Farm' at Chigwell (not demolished) where my Mother was born in 1884. Her Fiance was killed at Paschendale in World War One. He is named on the War Memorial in the Church Levi Mich Farrow.

My Mother was sympathetic with the Gypsies who were living on the common during her youth. They were driven off by the the local Authorities - but some stayed and lived in houses in the village. Their descendents still around when I was young. Aliens from the East End and Gypsies - nothing changes.

Crowds of people flocked to Chigwell Row at weekends, by bus, not car, and many little cottage Tea Shops existed - I believe my Aunt traded in the cottage where I live. Horse drawn buses brought children from the East End, pulling in at the 'Retreat' and at a large old wooden house nearer to the school.

'Pudding Lane' running off 'Gravel Lane' is the site old and new (ish) 'Burnt House'. The original destroyed by fire was the inspiration for 'Barnaby Rudge'. The old lane to Chigwell Village can still be traced beside it.

On this lane, 'Dolly Vardon' encountered 'Hugh the Ostler'. Later the rioting mob set fire to the house. Dickens 'Maypole Inn' was at Chigwell Row, later named 'Maypole Cottage' (demolished.).

Solomon Daisy hears the Church bell 'tolling across the fields' whilst drinking at the Inn. My ancestors, the Wederall's, kept the Inn during this time so maybe 'Jo Willet' was based on a bucolic ancestor of little brain. The Wederall tombstone near the entrance to Chigwell Row can still be seen.

'Woolhampton Way' commemorates the name of 'The Manor of Woolstenholme' which extended from Chigwell - I think to the Police Sports Ground. The story goes - I hope its true - that I am descended from the Lord of the Manor of Woolstenholme. A Daughter eloped with the handsome gardener. Discovering village life was distasteful, she was told 'you have made your bed and must lie on it'. I will end on this note hoping it gives you some ideas to inspire your creative writing.

PS. My Grandfather liked a drink, but it was the tipsy old lady, Grandmother of my prim and proper Sunday School teacher who fell out of the cart on the way home from Romford - he was obliged to go back and find her.

My Brown Owl - Dolly Wagstaff (C'est formidable).

Dave Williams - Shoe Mender - lived in the wooden cottages facing the old Bus Yard. His sweet-faced wife was a recluse, always hovering in the background.

Nobby Tridget - lived in an old railway carriage at 'Sunnymede' - he tended my Uncles pigs.

Ethel Pead - my elderly neighbour. With her Mother she cleaned the Church for many years. She deserves a long description: amongst many activities she studied form and backed many winners. She lived most of her life in a tiny cottage (now demolished) near J Shepherd.

BRAVE PEOPLE - I knew a lot about the personal struggles of those mentioned below, so am not prepared to discuss them, but realising I am creating a memorial different than that in the Church, I would like these people to be remembered as truly heroic 'Ordinary' people on my personal roll of honour.

Martha Lucas - Capstan Operator at Plesseys

Harry Lucas - Motor Mechanic

Anne Tipping - Drama and Elocution teacher, Sister of Mrs Bixby and Mother of courageous Michael.

Elsie's Story

I came here in 1946 from Bethnal Green to a house in Latchford Place. It was a far cry from East London and my first memories are that I got involved in Farm work. A lorry would pick a party of us up nearby and take us to Fowlers Farm at Pitsea.

There we worked on gathering sacks of corn, cutting rhubarb, tying the strings for runner beans and at the appropriate time, pulling the beans themselves.

I remember Thorns on the Industrial Estate where they manufactured wireless and television sets and my children were taught at Chigwell School.

There was to have been a further interview, but Elsie has moved from her recent accommodation in the Sheltered Housing in Manford Way to an unknown address.

Hainault Lodge Nature Reserve
By Les Chumley

Hainault Lodge was built in 1851 at the time the Deforestation of Hainault Forest.

Frederick Green JP, one time High Sheriff of Essex re-built the Lodge in the 1880's.

During the second world war, it housed officers from the Fairlop Airfield.

After the war, the house became Annex of Oldchurch Hospital. It remained derelict for 7 years, then it was finally demolished in 1973.

The site was acquired by the LBR in 1986 and enthusiastic volunteers from Havering and Redbridge Wildlife and Countryside Group began to manage the site in partnership with the Borough Nature Conservation Section.

It was the first Nature Reserve in LBR to be designated after consultation with the English Nature.

It was officially opened by Mayor Councillor Barden in 1995.

Today a Nature Trail has been constructed which allows visits from school parties through the reserve.

Side view of Hainault Lodge. 1913

Jack's Stories

Flight

In 1903 the Wright Brothers flew the first heavier than air plane at Kittyhawk.

In 1908 Alliot Verdon Roe landed a plane at Fairlop after flying it from a field that stood where the Ford Motor Company's Factory is now sited in Dagenham.

With his Brother Humphrey Verdon, he founded the aircraft firm of A V Roe and the company became Saunders Roe of Flying Boat building fame that designed and built the 'Saro'.

The site at Fairlop later became Fairlop Aerodrome and in World War Two, was a base for Hurricanes and Spitfires that took part in 'The Battle of Britain'.

Hainault Lodge

Where Forest Road meets Romford Road, the corner site that is now a Wildlife Sanctuary, it is shown on modern maps as 'Hainault Lodge'. The story is that in 1939 when World War Two broke out, it was thought Nazi Paratrooper's would come over as we fully expected them to invade us. So the building there, then an annexe to King Georges Hospital , was used to house the Princess's Margaret and Elizabeth. So if the expected danger arose they would be taken to a plane waiting at Fairlop Airfield to take them off to Canada.

At one time, open cast mining was carried out at Collier Row, hence the name. The house I live in is built above where the coal seams once were.

Related by Jack.

Jim Burns Story

Jim Burns Junior who with his two Brothers Robert and Thomas squatted on a piece of land at the top of the Lowe in Hainault and against the wishes of the local Councillors built an adventure playground which has remained as such since and is still in use by youngsters today. They also organised two Hainault Festivals on Elmbridge playing fields between 1973-1980.
Jim, who became a professional golfer, was also involved in planning the first European Golf Tournament in Cuba.

Hainault Creative Writers with Council Sponsorship have published three books and working with the pupils and Staff at Hainault County High and 'Spare Tyre Theatre Group' produced the material for a Wartime show 'Gas Mask On My Shoulder' and co acting with the pupils, the show was performed at the School, Community Centre, Ilford Town Hall, The Barbican and the Veterans tent at Hyde Park in 1995 to celebrate the end of World War 2.

Ken's Story

Although Ken now lives Chelmsford, he lived in Hainault before, during and after the Second World War and remembers well how things have changed.

The house he lived in was in New North Road opposite the building that was once 'Key Markets', but is now occupied by Barclays Bank and the P&O Line.

The New North Road was once named Chigwell Gardens.

From before the War, there was an old garage on the corner of New North Road and Tunstall Avenue owned by a Mr Cole, who was also the Leader of the local Boys Scouts. This building was demolished in the early 60's to make way for a Petrol Station that was demolished in 2001 and has since been replaced by a block of flats.

The corner of what is now Penrith Road was once a farm. This was sold off and houses were built there. The road at the time was Rowton Road, but for some reason it attracted a lot of undesirables and troublemakers, who were eventually cleared and the road was re-named Penrith.

The flats at Yellow Pine Way were built on what was once a part of Hainault Forest known as Butchers' Wood. There was a story that the wood was haunted and people wouldn't go through it at night.

The allotments in New North Road was once an area with cottages on. The man who lived there had been given the cottages and the land by his family who owned them. A 'Doodlebug' fell there during the war and later on the owner was found dead in one of the cottages.

The Railway Sidings in Hainault were taken over by the Americans during the War.

During the bombing raids, Hainault had its own mobile Ack, Ack Gun that roamed around Hainault firing at will whenever necessary, but moving continually.

During the bombing, a delayed action bomb fell in the garden of the house Ken lived in. At the time, they had an old bed to get rid of, so he and a mate, two young lads, unaware of the bombs presence dug a hole in the garden, placing the bed over the top to form a dug out. When his Father came home, he gave them a right telling off for digging in the garden as he knew there was a bomb there. Later, the Bomb Disposal

Squad came round and dug down 16ft in the garden, but couldn't find the bomb. They went away and came back the following week. This time they tunnelled in from the garden next door. This time they found it, de-fused it, and took it away.

Life was so uncertain during the War and possessions were cheap. Ken's Mother purchased half a house of furniture for the princely sum of just under £15.

A rocket fell in Dryden Close destroying houses at the bottom of the road. A woman was blown onto her Ascot water heater and her young baby was missing. The baby was later found unharmed 200 ft away from the explosion, upside down in a cradle.

EVACUATION
WORLD WAR II (1939-1945)
By Dan McMeekin

My brother and I were evacuated at the end of 1941 early 1942. We were dispatched from, I believe, Kings Cross railway station having suffered a bus journey from Dagenham where we lived, up through the blitzed streets of the East End. I remember that the streets were full of people milling around clearing up after maybe a recent air raid. There were fire engines and other vehicles dotted about and the path of the bus was over or around water hoses and debris, which was strewn all over the road and pavement.

I don't think our mum was with us. I have no recollection of the train journey, but nevertheless we arrived at Chesterfield. My brother, Tommy and I were paraded, with others, around the church hall complete with our labels pinned to our coats. We were chosen by a lady, I can't remember what she looked like, but she was quite plump. That evening the lady put us to bed. We didn't like the situation we were in and later made our escape. We were found wandering by a policeman and later at the police station during interrogation, and to the amusement of the officers present, when asked the reason for absconding, we replied that the lady had kissed us goodnight which was not acceptable since our mum didn't even do that.

The following morning we were placed with another family, namely the Stevenson's who lived at 15 Stores Road which is at a place called Brampton Terminus on the outskirts of the town. Standing in a certain position on the hill you can see the crooked spire of the church which Chesterfield is well known for. They treated us as one of the family as far as I can recall. They had two daughters who lived at home with them and I believe they had a son or sons who maybe was too old to serve in the war and he spent most of his time in the small holding at the back of the cottage. Every known species of vegetable was being grown in that garden and undoubtedly there was more than sufficient to supply the family with some to spare. The next door neighbour, who always wore a cap, was an apiarist with some 20 to 30 beehives dotted about his garden. I don't ever remember having any honey, so perhaps they were not on speaking terms, that would be funny with the country at war.

In addition to the vast vegetable plot, there was a large pen in which lived the biggest pig I have ever seen, well I was only five. This particular day, Mr Stevenson was mucking out the sty and he enlisted my assistance. When the sty door was fully open, it left a gap of about six inches between its edge and the fence. My job was to stand in the said opening so as to stop the pig from mounting an escape attempt. All kids are told old wives tales and this one was to the effect that if a pig's snout was to come into contact with your skin, it would keep sucking until you are dead - a terrible thought! The pig approached this small opening guarded by me, my courage failed me and I stepped back out of the way. This juggernaut, seizing its opportunity, made its bolt for freedom.

The onslaught that ensued was a sight to behold. This beast careered around the vegetable garden like the proverbial 'bull in a china shop'. Nothing or anything was spared, down came the runner beans and as it rampaged about with string and canes wrapped around it, the only sound apart from its crashing and bashing was the sound of the outraged Mr Stevenson shouting 'Damn you boy, Damn you'. The garden was complete devastation, everything churned and turned. For my sins I was incarcerated in the cellar, in complete darkness, for what seemed like eternity, I wasn't very happy. I was eventually rescued by Mrs Stevenson, a lovely lady. Needless to say, the old man and I didn't get on too well after that, or at least I was very wary of him. He once threatened to cut my hair with a massive pair of sheep shears. I'll never know if he was only joking. Other days were spent on a local farm. We were picked up each morning by one of the farm hands and enjoyed the trips on the horse and cart. We were there to assist in gathering in the harvest of whatever, but I suspect our contribution to the war effort was somewhat minimal.

Our mum came and visited us on one occasion, bringing our new sister with her, Elsie was only say, three months old, so that would be 1942. This idealist lifestyle eventually came to an end and we returned home. This coincided with the commencement of the dropping of the V1 'doodlebugs'. I don't think that it had anything to do with us returning, surely not. As kids, it was very exciting and from memory, a happy time. We were unofficial air aid wardens. Running up and down, knocking on doors in case of those who may not have heard the siren. Sitting under the front room dining table was second nature to us. On the all clear, we would venture out shrapnel collecting. Don't pick any up without holding your palm over the fragment to ensure that it had gone off the red hot, mistakes were made in our quest to get the biggest specimen.

My dad had sustained a fractured skull in a road accident and was deemed unfit for military service. As a consequence, he did more than his fair share because he served in the National Fire Service (NFS) and also the Home Guard. In the latter case he used to stand guard over the gun park, as we called it, which was situated over Parsloes Park, which is at Becontree, in Dagenham. The gun emplacements were about a quarter of a mile from where we lived and when they opened up during a raid the noise was absolutely deafening. My mum provided us with another brother, Billy, in 1944. The street party that we had to commemorate the end of the war in Europe, a photograph of which I have, shows us all. My mum is seen holding Billy in her arms and she is also heavily pregnant with my other sister Pat who was born in early 1946. Alas, she has now passed away, as has my dad who died in 1962 and my mum in 2001 aged 93 years. There were obviously plenty of kids produced during the war as in our family.

In 1997, some fifty four years later, I happened to be in the Chesterfield area and since the address is still in my memory, I called at 15 Stores Road. I pulled up in my car, just as a young woman came out to do something in the front garden. She looked somewhat perplexed when I introduced myself and explained the purpose of my visit. She invited me into the cottage, which had changed very little externally. She said they, her husband, had only recently purchased the cottage from the Stevenson family. I asked if I could go down into the cellar for a moment. Having turned off the light, certain memories came flooding back, a very moving experience. On entering the back garden, I was disappointed to find just a wilderness. I told her what it was like all that time ago and some of the experiences that we had had. The trellis covered with pink roses, which I remember was just outside the back door, was gone. She said that her husband had recently taken it down. Surely it could not have been that same trellis and climbing rose after all that time?

I'm glad I called that day. I'll probably never call again, but will forever remember, with fondness and a little sadness, those days spent in Derbyshire past and present.

23rd June 2003

Hainault Forest
By Beryl Risbridger

The first glimpse I had of Hainault Forest was just before the War when my Junior School arranged a trip there and thence on to Epping Forest. We were transported in some sort of charabanc, as coaches were known then.

Born and bred in Barking, where the biggest open ground was the park, the forest seemed huge. It's amazing how one's perception of size then is so different than that of an adult.

We were dropped off at a large, barn-like building with all sorts of animal heads adorning the walls. I found it quite creepy!

We broke up into groups and started exploring. There were hundreds of blackberry bushes everywhere and dense trees. We discovered the lake hidden away, exactly where it is today, with children sitting along the edge holding crudely made rods with bits of string for fishing lines and others with fishing nets and jam jars for catching tiddlers. Years later I took my own children and also my grand children to do the self-same thing.

However, much to our teacher's displeasure, we managed to get lost! Years later it was still difficult to get from where I lived to the forest. Having no car, we used to either ride our bikes or walk from the Hawbush Pub, which was as far as the 62 bus went then.

At the top of Hog Hill there was a five bar gate, which was the entrance to the forest, leading to the blackberry bushes where we used to collect delicious fruit. Sadly, these were eventually destroyed and now there are just open pastures, depriving the children of all the fun of playing hide and seek.

The last time I visited the forest, there were two large parking areas, full of cars, a farm and wide open areas for walking, but somehow lacking the excitement of finding your way around all the trees and bushes and even panicking when you thought you were lost.

If you went by bike with sandwiches and a bottle of drink, you could spend a whole day there without it costing you a penny.

Sadly, nowadays it is not very safe to ride a bike, nor to let children play unfettered in parks and forests.

Such is the price of 'progress'??

16/8/05

Once Upon A Time
By George Duffree

Our first meeting was on Wanstead Flats Easter Fair in 1935. We dated for twelve months and decided to get engaged.

As we had both come from poor cramped living conditions in Leyton and Leytonstone, we agreed to start saving money to get enough for our future home.

As Kay had been in live in service from 14 years of age and was now used to living in very good conditions, we both wanted to look forward to a very good lifestyle.

It took us two years to save ONE hundred pounds, in sixpence or shillings a week, or whatever we could afford.

In the mean time, we purchased a tandem to save on fares as my wages were only three pounds a week. So that did not leave me much pocket money after I paid for my keep at home.

In January 1938 we started to look in local papers for properties to let. All we could find were two rooms or damp basement flats.

As I was in the building trade, through the grapevine I heard that another firm were building new maisonettes in Hainault off of New North Road. We arranged a meeting with the Estate Agent in Tomswood Hill who took us by car to the site, but miles around Chigwell before Dryden Close. We thought Hainault was the last place God made.

We were overjoyed to be offered a brand new maisonette and have the pick of all the finished properties, so we chose No.34a first floor. We could now plan our Wedding Day and with the money we had saved, we will be able to furnish our home with all new items.

Now we had the pleasure to go shopping to buy the furniture. (1) Table, four chairs and sideboard cost ten pounds. (2) Bedroom suite complete cost twenty two pounds (3) A three piece hide suite cost twenty five pounds (4) To cover all floors cost three pounds ten shillings for linoleum and mats.

Now was the time to find our way about Hainault. The 150 bus had a turn bay opposite The Maypole Public House in Fencepiece Road.

As we walked down New North Road the houses and shops were as they are today, down as far as Kelvin Hughes Factory. Opposite was their large canteen and from there were only one or two houses until the Railway Station and cottages. The railway arch across the road at the time was very low.

The steam trains running at the time were one each hour between Ilford and Woodford. The shops outside the station are the same today, still walking down the road houses were on both sides until you reach the allotments. The houses on the left finished and it was open fields right up to Manor Road, Chigwell.

On the right hand side from the allotments were six farm cottages where the Bank now stands. The bungalows went on as far as Newcastle Road. From there, New North Road was just a country farm track with grass growing in the wheel tracks as far as the Hainault Oak Public House.

Where the garage at Elmbridge corner used to be was a farm where we used to buy our milk, eggs and pick mushrooms in the fields.

After the war, we were informed that a new estate was going to be built by the L.C.C. for the overspill of London.

The main contractors were W C French. The first road to be laid was Manford Way, then all the various roads from it. Owing to the number of men employed on this large contract, the first building had to be the men's canteen. It is still there and called Frenchies canteen in the Hainault Community Centre.

The men needed transport, so the company laid on a single deck bus that could pass under the low bridge. This bus turned round at Covert Road, later on at the Lowe.

So Hainault began to expand. First the shops in Manford Way, then the road under the railway bridge was lowered to be able to get a double decker bus on the 150 route, which today still runs from Ilford to Chigwell.

17/10/03

Rita Tappenden's Story

Born in East Ham Rita's family moved to Leytonstone and were there at the height of the Blitz. The air raid siren had gone and Rita's Uncle and Aunt took refuge in an Anderson Shelter while Rita, her mum and dad dived into the coal cupboard under the stairs.

A bomb fell close to the house killing her uncle and aunt in the shelter but Rita and her parents were safe in the coal cupboard although her father was injured and lost one of his good eyes, her mother and herself were not hurt.

After that shocking experience she felt unable to carry on with her wartime job at Cossor's Factory helping to make bombs and went to Panfield near Braintree where she became a Milkmaid.

Her future husband was a Japanese Prisoner of War and spent three and a half years at the infamous prisoner of war camp at Changi in Singapore and was forced to work on the railway of death where so many of our men died in the building of it.

He survived the terrible cruelties of the Japanese and Rita was told by another who was with him at the time that, a letter she had sent him to say they were engaged helped to see him through his ordeal. On his return at the end of the war they were married.

They moved to Hainault 45 years ago, to Sylvester Gardens, her eldest daughter Anne went to Warren School, Pat her youngest first attended Coppice, then went to Kingswood, as the school was called at that time. Kingswood is now Hainault County High.

Rita became involved with Hainault Golf Course where she discovered that the club house was once a School and the old bell that was used to summon the children to school was made by Mears and Stainbank of London in 1885, it now hangs in the club's main lounge. The club itself was opened in 1912.

Before the old Hainault Oak pub was pulled down (The one before the one that was demolished recently) there were a row of very old cottages alongside it. A friend of hers lived in one of the cottages and at that time they only had gas for lighting and heating. The cottages were demolished in 1971 along with the old pub and new houses built in their place.
10/05/04

Mrs Nemo's Story

Born in Tyne Road Ilford, her parents moved to Greenwood Gardens in 1930 when she was two. The School she attended was Fairlop the one that is now 'The Music Centre' in Fencepiece Road. At that time the School was being built and only the building at the back was finished and in use as a permanent structure The Main building in the front was still being built.

Her classes were mainly held in a temporary building they called 'The Hut' which was in the playground by the gate.

A woman known as Blind Flory lived in a house by an empty plot of land in Fencepiece Road from a tall box laden with sweets she stood outside the school gates selling sweets and goodies to the children when they came out of school for a Farthing or Halfpenny a time. She was acute and no one could catch her for anything, blind or not.

There were no buses running then and everyone had to walk to school but children were a bit envious of two girls from Tunstall Avenue who were taken to and from school by horse-drawn carriage. At one time Mr Edmund's was Headmaster at Fairlop School and a fete was organised for a Saturday. He told his son about it and his son was Noel Edmund's, he announced the event over the radio. So many people turned up for the occasion, that on the day the organisers found the numbers were almost too much to cope with, although everything turned out well in the end.

Stedman's wood yard was on the corner of Maypole Crescent and it was a popular place for youngsters. When it was closed they used to hop over the fence to hunt for snakes which were plentiful among the timber.

The first eight houses at the top of New North Road belonged to him and were the residences of his family members.

Her Grandparents lived in Stoke Cottages off Tomswood Hill, a line of dwellings that had no party walls dividing the lofts and an Uncle who was in the Navy brought home a Monkey from abroad that managed to escape into the loft spaces and ran riot and led everyone a right old dance until it was eventually caught.

Her grandfather used to walk every morning from his house to Fairlop School to give her a bar of Nestles chocolate before she went to class.

They also had a Parrot that seemed to keep an eye on her. If she tried to sneak out of the house without her mother knowing the Parrot would scream out "She's got her hat on" and that was the end of her outing. Her other Grandmother owned the farm opposite Jusums Lane, Romford, named 'Lowlands'. When the farm was eventually sold, a condition of the sale was that the name should still be carried on and Lowland Gardens is there today.

Her Grandmother kept a big fierce dog that only she could handle, it was kept in a kennel outside. It had no name and was just called 'Dog'; She sold her produce from the farm in Romford Market. When she returned with the money in a bag she kept it in the safest place she knew, in with the dog, as no one dared go near it.

Her father and Uncle were in the Royal Horses Artillery and her father rode the lead horse on a Gun Carriage.

Where a row of shops are in Tomswood Hill by Barkingside roundabout the shops before the present ones were built in their place there was from left to right Coles Tea Shop, Sawtons the Butcher, Crawleys the Snobs (boot and shoe repairers) and Hunt's the Greengrocers.

'The Maypole' was on the site where 'Fags and Mags' is now located and when it was demolished with the original shops the pub moved to it's present location in Fencepiece Road opposite New North Road and the 'Fairlop Oak' was built where it is now on the roundabout.

In Barkingside itself, by the side of the old Police Station was a 'Smithy' owned by a Mr George Wall. This was demolished along with the old Police Station and the latest one when built was extended into where the old Old Smithy was.

Across the road where McDonalds and Iceland now stand was a garden centre that extended along Mossford Green.

At the beginning of the war in 1939 one of her neighbours was called up for the Army and their Anderson shelter hadn't been installed in the garden, so a hole had to be dug to put it in. When he left to do his Service he instructed his three sons to do it. They managed it and everything seemed ok until one day their mother had to take shelter. She jumped down into it and much to her surprise and with a bit of a shock she found herself waist deep in cold water.

Unknowingly the lad's had broken through a water pipe running beneath the garden. To get to it the shelter had to be taken out and placed in another part of the garden.

When the bombing started in 1940 she was evacuated to the country until she reached the age of fourteen when she had to return to Hainault for 'War Work'. It was just at the time the Doodlebugs (VI's). Followed later by the Rockets (V2's) that started to fall on London and around. She got a job at Kelvin Hughes as a coil winder. This work was carried out in the 'Manor Hall' in Manor Road that had been converted into a factory to help with the War effort. When an air raid warning sounded they had to run across the road and sit in a ditch to take shelter, as no proper air raid shelter was available. She worked there for two years until she contracted yellow jaundice brought on by the work and was then signed off medically unfit for work.

Her next job was as a projectionist at the 'Super Cinema' in Ilford, it was staffed completely by women as all the men had been called up for the Forces. The Cinema was bombed and she was struck in the head by the metal chimney that carried away the fumes from the projector and knocked unconscious.

The 'Super' was a wreck so she went on to the' Savoy' Cinema at Gants Hill as a projectionist staffed mainly by women with a few young lads. There were many American troops in the Ilford area and they were regular visitors to the cinemas.

Part of the playing fields towards Barkingside, at the back of Saltash Road was called the 'Prairie' and a heavy anti-aircraft gun was installed there. Every time it fired, the blast broke all the windows in the area except for her parents house in Maypole Crescent. Her dad put that down to a massive Magnolia tree that grew in the front of the house absorbing all the blast.

There was also mobile anti aircraft guns that roamed the streets firing at will leaving behind their trail of broken windowpanes.

When war in Europe came to an end , crowds of people were out on the streets cheering, singing and dancing to celebrate the end of the war but the cinema of the Savoy couldn't be out with them as there were two customers still there determined to finish watching the programme. The show had to go on regardless.

As our troops began to liberate parts of Eastern Europe the first films showing the horrors of the Concentration Camps were being shown at the 'Savoy' and other cinemas. The terrible scenes shown were completely unbelievable and were a terrific shock to the population as a whole, as no one ever knew these horrors were being perpetrated.

The Cinema staff however, being subjected to having the news screened twice a day, seven days a week found the experience even more traumatic.

Before the estate around Tomswood Hill was built a number 25 bus service started to run through to 'The Beehive' as the 'Camelot' was named. The route was via Colvin Gardens.

Buses couldn't travel the length of New North Road as the bridge at Hainault Station was too low. it wasn't until the war ended that it was rectified and Italian Prisoners of War billeted in the London Transport Depot were used to dig out the road below the bridge, sufficient to allow the double decker bus to get under.

After the war she got married and her husband and herself moved into one of the many Prefabricated Houses that were being erected all over Britain as an emergency measure to fill the tremendous gap of the housing shortage caused by the devastation of wartime bombing and the V1's and V2's. They were intended as temporary structures to last twenty-five years to allow more permanent houses to be built. Many of them were still lived in thirty to forty years later.

Their Pre-Fab was in Woodman Road in Hainault and they thought that living in a Pre-Fab was brilliant, designed by a Swedish woman architect who knew the sort of places most women wanted.

Pre-Fab's had everything, they were laid out in a modern way and the kitchen had built in cupboards, bathroom's with a proper bath ect and spacious rooms. with gas fired heating, they were most comfortable. Single storied structures made of Asbestos panels, had flat roofs, metal doors, window frames and space around them for a garden. They proliferated everywhere. Time rolled by and came the day when the Pre-Fab's were all to be removed and the residents were to be rehoused by the council. Although she didn't want to leave her home they had no choice.

All the occupants had a chance to buy their Pre-Fab but they had to find a plot of ground to re-erect it on. Her husband and herself were interested in this and looked around to see if they could find themselves a plot.

Her husband talking to a man living in Tomswood Hill was told by him there was a plot that had been vacant for years at the back of some old cottages off the hill and Mossford Lane. It looked really promising and when they went to the Council Offices requesting permission to build on the site, they were told the plot didn't exist. Immediately after their request they found the Council had stepped in and claimed the land for the Council.

Having lived in a Pre-Fab for so many years they only wanted to move into a Bungalow and they found what they were looking for in Tunstall Avenue. The front room had been used as a car repair shop and the fireplace that turned out to be a really lovely red brick design, was blackened beyond recognition by soot from oily rags that had been burnt in the grate.

There was seven old cars in the garden that had to be got rid of, but with all the problems her husband was able to see the potential of the place and after a lot of hard work he turned it into a home that anyone would be proud of.

As they settled in they dug for a fish pond and lo and behold, buried in the garden was another old car. They couldn't do much with that but had to re-locate the position of the pond.

The row of bungalows where she lived had gates at the back and the deeds of the house contained a clause that the gate had to be retained to allow a farmer in the vicinity to have access to drive his pigs through the the gates were still there until it was obvious they would no longer be required.

The bungalow next door had been empty for years and a massive Cherry tree had grown up in the garden over the years. In the big storm of 1987 it was blown down, but fell in such a way that it landed between a shed and a greenhouse without doing any damage to either of them.

30.12.04.

The Old Chequers Inn, Barkingside 1928

J. Middleton - Blaney 1978

High Street, Barkingside 1927

A. Middleton - Blaney 1979

The Old Maypole,
Broadway, Barkingside.
1927

THE OLD MAYPOLE, BROADWAY, BARKINGSIDE. 1927.

A. Middleton - Blaney 1977

A. Middleton - Blaney 1977

New Fairlop Oak P.H.
Barkingside 1906

Police Station & Smithy
Barkingside 1904

POLICE STATION & SMITHY 1904
BARKINGSIDE

J. BRITTON 1982

J. Britton 1982

Hainault my Hainault
By Stan Murray

This is an East Ender's potted version of how the sleepy suburban village of Hainault became a cultural extension of the East End of London and also how it became my home. The cultural changes however were not wholly one way, for some of the suburban cultures rubbed out on us. In the early transitional days, when an East Ender opened his mouth, his cockney accent immediately gave him away. Now after fifty years of integration, the traditional cockney dialect has all but faded into obscurity, especially among the younger generation.

I met my present wife Eleanor (but she was nicknamed Nell) in 1947 when we were living in Hackney, East London. I had recently been de-mobbed from the Army after serving nine years in various theatres of war including, India, Burma, Malaya and French Indo China (Vietnam now of course). I was finding it really hard to settle down for I was missing the comradeship and stimulation of Army life.

After Nell and I had been together for about three months, I re-enlisted for the army, Nell was utterly devastated, for we had become very close. I still can't believe that I could have done such a thing to a lovely girl like Nell, but those were young and foolish years. I still think now, how could I have done such a thing? I signed up for three years, However two months before my release date was due, the Korean war started and all demob was halted, it was another eighteen months before my demob date finally came through, but I'm glad to say, Nell waited for me.

Nell and I had been writing regularly to each other when she wrote that her family had moved to a place in Essex called Hainault. It was a new London County Council estate just on the outskirts of London. The next time I went on leave, Nell met me at Liverpool Street Station with the usual hugs and kisses, but seemed a bit on edge - nervous like. Hainault of course is at the end of the Central Line and as we travelled along we left the congested buildings and narrow streets of London and entered the green fields and fresh air of the countryside. At that time there were cattle grazing in the fields.

The journey took about twenty five minutes and I really enjoyed it.

When we came out at Hainault Station, there was a bus stop opposite, I looked at the timetable attached to the post and said to Nell, "What's the date?" When she told me I said, "So today's an odd day, the buses only run on even days." I was being funny, Nell always had a good sense of humour, but this time she didn't appear to enjoy the joke and said, "We can walk, it's not far." it took about twenty minutes to walk to Burrow Road where Nell lived and she was more or less silent as we walked along, which was very uncharacteristic of her, The estate was so new that some of the new houses were not yet occupied, while others were in the process of being built. Her house was at the end of a small block of solidly built brick houses which had both front and rear gardens. Her parents told me they loved the place, but said Nell didn't, she had told them she missed her mates and wanted to go back. She was also getting rather rebellious, which was totally out of character, Even with me she didn't seem her normal self, but contrary to what her parents said, Nell told me how nice it was there with the pub only ten minutes away and only twenty five minutes to London. Then the penny dropped. Nell was concerned that I wouldn't like it there and would go back to London. I also remembered that on the train as we were travelling to Hainault, Nell said a few times, "It's not far now." No wonder she didn't enjoy that remark about the buses running only on even dates.

I didn't say anything right away, but in the evening when we were in the pub I said "this is a nice pub isn't it ? I like these old world pubs" Nell said "Do you". I said "Yes, this is a nice place Hainault, it's sort of out in the country, I've got to like the country since I've been in the army and I don't think I'd like to go back to London really." We were sitting side by side on a small bench seat and Nell turned to me, her big brown eyes open in amazement exclaiming, "What! You like it here?" I looked at her with some concern on my face and said. "What's the matter? You're not thinking of going back to London are you?" She threw her arms around me exclaiming loudly "No--O" I don't know what the other people in the pub thought I was doing to her, we laughed about it afterwards, I'd got the Nell I knew back again.

Us Londoner's, many of whom were from the East End brought a part of the East End with us. Introducing music in the pubs, with the customers getting up and singing on the mikes, there were also talent

competitions and jellied eel stalls. Every morning before 7.30 there could be seen workers scurrying towards Hainault station, joining in the morning ritual of arriving before 7.30, this was in order to buy half price
workman's ticket. There would also be a rush to get in the queue for a ticket before 7.30, but the majority of people made sure they arrived in good time. Even the buses would wait for people hurrying along to catch them, the conductors knew all the commuters and a great deal of good humoured banter went on between them. Most people retained their jobs in London where they had previously worked comparatively close to home. So this commuting business on the crowded tube trains was completely alien to them and to say the least, unpleasant.
Apart from this, the majority of married adults fell in love with their new houses and also with the new environment, but the children and young single adults, well, I don't think resentment would be too harsh an adjective to describe their feelings. I suppose you could see their point, they had left all their friends behind, some had to find new schools and others maybe new jobs, then in addition to this, had visions of country bumpkins to contend with. You see, as far as they were concerned, they had been content with their lot in London, yet had now been callously separated from the surroundings and friends they knew and loved so well, then dumped in the country somewhere, in a place called Hainault. But all was not so bad as it first appeared. The children were first to recognise this and also the first to benefit from it. They joined the local schools and found the locals were remarkably like themselves, they met other children who came from the East End and also found that there were more things to do here, like lakes to fish in, the forest and parks to play in . Therefore integration for them was not so long in coming.
But for single adults it was rather a different story, especially for those who were romantically involved and had to leave their other half behind. However when they found how easily and quickly it was to to London , the blow was softened somewhat - but not much. The evenings and weekends were the worst, especially for the girls, who missed their close friends. For back home they would go dancing, or have a drink and a chat in a pub, or visit each others homes, now all that was gone. However, those who worked in London were fortunate in the fact

that they regularly travelled backwards and forwards on the tube and therefore made new friends, but unfortunately there was no place they could all meet and get to know each other.

But help in resolving the problem was at hand, for building work on the Estate was still in progress. The building workers had a canteen on the site called French's canteen, so the site manager was approached with the view to allowing the young adults to meet there in the evenings. He obtained the necessary permission, and the problem solved.

Nell and I were still writing to each other and in one of her letters she wrote that she had settled down in Hainault and was going around with a group of friends her own age. Now, in situations such as were occurring in Hainault, where it was both males and females who felt lonely and isolated, any group that formed would almost certainly be mixed, consisting of both males and females. Also, in a group such as this, it is natural for couples to pair off - Umm!! Nell was good looking and very popular, with a quiet unassuming personality that drew people to her, so I was naturally concerned regarding the outcome of all this.

So in order to spice up my army life, I had joined the Para -Yes--ss!, that spiced it up alright. When I came home on my first leave from Germany, I met the members of the group that Nell had palled up with. It was on a Saturday night in the long bar of the Maypole Pub, Chigwell Row. Nell introduced me and the group were suitably impressed, which I intended them to be. I was in uniform wearing my red beret with my parachute wings on my right shoulder and below them the crossed swords of a PTI (Physical Training Instructor). I also had five medal ribbons on my left chest denoting my wartime theatres of operations. I smiled and said hello! then, unnoticed by Nell, gave each of the males a short meaningful gaze - hands off! We went out with the group a few times during my leave and other times when I came home on leave, and although I got on well with all of them, I couldn't help feeling that some of the lads secretly wished that I'd find a Fraulein and stay out in Germany. Anyway, the next time I came home on leave, Nell and I became engaged - fait accompli.

They were halcyon days, coming home on leave, meeting Nell at Liverpool Street Station, going to the Maypole, singing on the mike. But then, as always, I had to go back. It became that much harder - for both of us. When my term of service expired, I was asked to sign on for a further term, but declined. The attraction of army life was no longer there. Nell and I married in 1953 and I carried on singing around the pubs - still do, in the Working Man's Club in New North Road, sometimes to Nell's embarrassment.

So, that's why I still love 'Hainault my Hainault'

Beryl's Story

My parents were from Cornwall and moved to Collier Row in 1931 when my Sister was ten and I was four years old. They had bought a new house in Riversdale Road which was part of a small estate of about five roads.

Collier Row then was a small village and when my Mother opened a Post Office account for me, the number was 'Collier Row 301'.

From the back bedroom window were wonderful views of just fields and a rambling River Rom, which became my playground. We could walk from our back garden for hours and never pass another person or any habitation.

My Sister started school at the Church of the Ascension School that came under the Diocese of Chelmsford. It had two classrooms and a Headmaster's study; the heating provided by a boiler in the centre of the classroom and toilets Elsan type were in the playground. The Headmaster lived in a house alongside the school.

The old building is still there near the 'City Limits' bowling centre and the garden centres at the beginning of Collier Row Lane. The old building is now called 'The Oaks' that became a centre for young people, but is now closed as the front of the building is now in danger of collapsing.

As the school was about a two mile walk and we came home to lunch (no school dinners in those days), I must have walked about eight miles a day as a five year old. We did, however, have a long break from 12noon to 2pm.

On the way to school, we would pass the local Blacksmith and would stop to see the horses being shod. This old forge was on the corner of White Hart Lane on the opposite corner of the old 'White Hart' Pub. This building was demolished to build a new 'White Hart', that itself has recently been demolished.

One of our family walks was along Clockhouse Lane, which was then a small country lane with a Clockhouse at the top and on to the Pinewoods and Havering-Atte-Bower.

I remember my Father saying to me 'that when I was grown up and had children of my own, there would be houses in Clockhouse Lane'. Within just a few years (about 1938), his words came true and we watched the 'Nash Estate' being built and also the Clockhouse Lane School, where I became one of its first pupils.

In the summer we swam in the Havering open air pool in Orange Tree Hill. We cycled or walked everywhere as the only cars were owned by a 'Rich Uncle'. We sometimes had a bus trip to Romford, the fare one penny to see the cattle on market days.

Most of the summer we spent with a jam jar and a net, fishing and falling in the magical River Rom. Often we walked across the fields to Hainault Forest which I grew to love and still do.

The Ascension Church Hall was the centre of our social life. It was also the local library where the books were kept behind wiring until 'Library Day'. It was there I joined Sunday School, the Brownies, the Youth Club and where my Sister and I were married. Oh Happy Days.

The site where 'City Limits' is now, was during the Second World War an open field that housed an Ack, Ack gun. The men who manned it were billeted in the area. The gun was fired many times during air raids and the next day my Sister and I would comb the area searching for pieces of shrapnel that came from the shells that exploded in the air.

Photo One, is of a sports day held in the fields behind Riversdale Road, now the 'Nash Estate' in 1936 to celebrate the Coronation of King George the Sixth after the abdication of King Edward. The local people contributed one penny a week each to pay for their day.

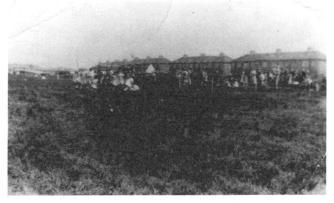

1936 Coronation Sports Day

Photo Two, shows the open fields beyond Riversdale Road

Photo Three, shows people making the most of the open air.
Barking and Dagenham Council now own the building, but boat repairs
are now carried out in the grounds.

A CHANGE IN TIME AT THE MAYPOLE CHIGWELL
By Jim Burns

I was looking at two photos, one dated 1931, the other one 1976, both taken outside The Maypole Inn, Chigwell.

Photo No 1 1931. The scene of tranquillity is evident, the pub had a pond along side it, a few men were fishing, it is a Saturday morning, the sun shone warm. The smell of Honeysuckle wafted in the warm breeze, the bells of Chigwell Church rang out it's message across the fields to the cottages in Hainault.

Standing outside The Maypole a line of men with the local constable with his bicycle all smiling at the camera man, they were waiting for the Charabanc to take them to Southend for the day, for this is Mayday the workers day.

Just beyond the pond on the common, stood a high pole striped in red and white, with long straps hanging down all in red and white, which will soon have happy laughing children dressed in their Sunday best clothes swinging around the Maypole to the music from the old organ grinder. Picnics will soon be laid out around the common and soon Dr Ross, an old eccentric land owner will be driving his miniature steam engine full of happy children around the common. In the Maypole pub the air thick with the smell of beer, tobacco and sawdust, men were singing to the music from the piano.

The sun has set on this time in history.

Photo No 2 1976 The Maypole has been rebuilt; a large sign hangs down, stating that Charles Dickens stayed there as he wrote Barnaby Rudge. The pond has gone, in it's place a concrete car park, the common has gone now a housing estate, Chigwell Church bells has stopped ringing, unless a marriage has been arranged, the bells are extra. The photo shows a group of young men standing outside the Maypole pub, dressed in flared trousers, psychedelic coloured shirts, long hair resting on their shoulders, a policeman is talking to them, he is holding a an Alsatian dog on a lead, the dog is sniffing for drugs. Music from the Maypole is blasting out. 'Lucy in the Sky with Diamonds'. Across the road The Retreat public house, oldie worldly type, this was the hub of the the new well off youth showing off with fast cars and pints of larger, local celebrities, Bobby Moore, Jeff Hurst, Charlie George to name but a few who would frequent 'The Retreat' 'helping to put Hainault

Hainault on the map. Because just down the road is the Hainault Estate, built just after the 1939/45 war, when the Labour Party won a landslide election victory. The London County Council built the houses fit for heroes, two and three bedrooms, large gardens, tree lined streets, Community Centre, shops and schools and hundreds of Prefabs for temporary housing.

Then in 1990 a fault was found in the houses, a building company called Swans rebuilt the estate, removing the drab grey cladding, replacing them with various shades of red brick, it really transformed the appearance of The Hainault Estate.

The Hainault Kids
By Marion Osborn

Jimmy Greaves was the Wayne Rooney of his day! He was also a Hainault kid. I'd never ever heard of Hainault until I moved to Dagenham. Our family was part of the great over-spill, from the London slums to suburbia , which to us town dwellers seemed like the country. At first I was thrilled and delighted with our new house and looked forward to settling into our new environment and making lots of new friends. We were quickly disillusioned!

As cockney kids, we were looked down on for being not only common but also dirty. It was generally known that we did not have bathrooms where we came from. We were ridiculed for using the bath to keep coal in, because it was assumed we didn't have a clue as to it's correct purpose. I never met anyone who actually did do this, and we certainly didn't.

Common? Well we couldn't help the way we spoke! Anyway, they weren't that posh themselves. As to dirty, we washed in the tin bath in the kitchen every Friday without fail, whether we needed it or not, and for special treats went to the public baths when Mum had the money. So you can imagine, we felt like outcasts and really missed our old home, where everybody was on the same level as us.

Our new school, South Wood Lane, was actually in our road and it wasn't long before we noticed coaches pulling in every morning and children piling off and running into school. They were Hainault Kids being bused in because they didn't have a school to go to where they lived.

Like me they seemed set apart and I warmed to them. I felt more of an affinity with them than I ever did for the snooty and unfriendly kids where I now lived, I loved to watch them play footer in the playground and particularly one of them who was an absolute wizard. He was Greavsie, who later went on to play for England and was in the squad that won the World Cup in 1966.

I wanted very much to go to this 'Hainault'. It seemed a more friendly and welcoming place somehow. One day my kid sister and I did just that.

We set off on our great adventure with my bike and her one roller skate between us, and taking turns on them, followed the bus route. When we finally arrived we found it was the 'proper' country. it had a huge forest and everything! We absolutely loved it and often went there afterwards and made friends with the local children, less laboriously than on our first visit, however, as by then my sister had acquired her own bike.

Since then I have always had a soft spot for Hainault and now a senior citizen, I am a member of the Writers Group that meets every week at the Hainault Forest Community Centre. So I have come full circle and young at heart, still think myself very much as being, by adoption, a 'Hainault Kid'

Who Is Hainault? What Is She?
By John Bartholomew

In 1949 a letter came from the L.C.C. informing us that we would be considered for a council house in a place called Hainault in Essex. Our first reaction was, where the bloody hell is that? Nobody knew, nobody had ever heard of the place but finally we traced it on the Underground Tube Map as a place near Gants Hill at the end of the Central Line. We eventually managed to get there from where we lived in the West End of London.

As we walked from Hainault Station we passed many prefabs built during the war and they looked depressing.

Finally after ploughing through unmade streets of yellow clay, we found the never to be forgotten Rent's Office. Peopled by the escapees from the recently disbanded Gestapo. Although minus the Jackboots, their attitude was the same, but they resisted using the word Schnell for the more English "Well, what do you want?" However they did point us in the direction of the house we were to view and where we have lived since.

As a Trolley Bus driver in London I was able to transfer to the Depot that existed in Ley Street, Ilford.

The people in Ilford in those days were principally retired Civil Servants, aping their erstwhile Employers and owing the expected Mortgage, without two halfpennies to jingle on a tombstone.

There were no bus request stops in those days and if a retired person shot out from the side as a bus was passing, shaking an umbrella or a walking stick for the bus to stop, one was supposed to stand the bus on it's head to humour him. Should he take your number you could be suspended or lose a days pay.

Chigwell, Woodford and Ilford bitterly resented the incursion of the common folk of London to the Hainault Estate. It must have been a terrible shock to their susceptibilities. Not withstanding, the wealth, experience and reality they brought to the area.

I remember on one occasion attending a meeting of the council at Ilford Town Hall where the Bovine type struggled to her feet and uttered the following----" Mr Chairman Sir. Are you aware that some of those people on that Hainault Estate actually have Motor Cars?"

I was obliged to walk out .

I am forced to ask the question once again; Where is Hainault? What is Hainault? Is there such an address?
Apart from the station it does not exist.

Bordered on one side by Woodford, another Chigwell and then Ilford.
What is She?
She is indeed a fragment of the imagination of the toffee-nosed old Ilfordians? Substituting the high-faluting name of Hainault?, for the more practical name known at the time as Train Halt.

My First School
By Paul Silverman

The late 1950's and early 60's were good times for going to infants and junior school.
The back gate of Manford Way school was just a walk away and eventually my mother stopped taking me. I'd wander along with school friends. The type of lessons were probably different to now (2004) as we started to learn to read and write. We learned to write using pens with nibs which we dipped in the inkwells.
It sounds like the nineteenth century, yet it was just forty years ago.

More important to me in later life, it was during this period that my interest in reading and in history developed. That deepened until eventually I experienced the Open University and after years of part time study I was awarded an honours degree in Humanities. I am jumping ahead.
Often after school was over, friends would come home and have a bite of tea and play in the back garden or in the house or I would go with someone else back to their home. Inevitably I would be told off for going without telling my mother- she warned about strangers - but it was a sign of the times that we felt safe and we were innocent of what could happen. The other side of the coin is that the time at junior school had it's moments when I had difficulties, especially as it was during this period that my disability began to show itself and for a while nobody knew what was happening to me.
Fortunately in 1964 it was diagnosed as I had started secondary school in Becontree Heath in what was then known as a Technical school. I'm not certain of the difference between 'technical' and 'grammar' school at this time, we still needed to pass the 'eleven plus' to qualify. At the time the Secondary Modern that I would have gone to, had I failed the eleven plus, was "Grange" in Manford Way at the bottom of Tine Road. This has gone now.

21/06/04

Paul's Story

Handicapped from the day he was born his story is one of courage. Up to a few weeks old, hospital staff wouldn't allow his Mother to see him as they said although he was a strong baby, so early they had branded him as an imbecile. How wrong they were. 'Strong' was the key word for his mind and spirit in the way he overcame his afflictions created mainly by what was later to be defined as Cerebral Palsy.

Born in Ilford his family lived in Swaffham Road.

During the Second World War when the bombing, V1's and V2's had destroyed so many houses, something had to be done to provide homes quickly. The answer was the 'Pre-Fab'. Built of asbestos and steel, they were large square single storey structures with flat roofs and placed on a concrete foundation. They had two bedrooms, a living room, bathroom and kitchen.

When three years old, Paul's family moved to No.2 Kennylands Road near Forest Road into one of the many Pre-Fabricated houses that had been built around the Hainault Estate. In addition there were others built in Manford Way and New North Road. Moving into a single storey structure made access easier for Paul.

Cattle on the way to Romford were driven past their door as they were taken to the thriving Cattle Market that was there at the time. The space now taken up by stall holders or car park was then criss-crossed with cast iron pens to hold the animals.

Pre-Fabs were comfortable dwellings, but in the hard winter of 1962, when a hard freeze lasted for ten weeks, Paul's Dad had to use a hammer and chisel to get the metal front door open of a morning as it was frozen solid. They were ideal homes, but were only supposed to last for ten years. Many of them however went on well past that time, but when tenants had to get out they were sorry to leave.

When the homes were dismantled, it was done very carefully and they were taken off for another destination, Billy Butlin's Holiday Camps.

By the age of three Paul had measles three times and at four years Scarlet Fever.

He attended various schools in Ilford starting at a nursery school when he was three.

He was a passenger on the school bus with other children on board and surprised everyone when the driver of the mini bus collapsed at the wheel as he was pulling out and Paul had the sense to go to the front of the bus and turn off the ignition.

He suffered regular fits, two to three a day, but was determined he wouldn't let them get him down.

At five years old he was taken regularly to Great Ormond Street Hospital for manipulation and at that age could play Chess.

When he was six, there was talk of fitting him with Callipers, which even at that age he was determined he wouldn't wear them.

At fourteen he was getting bad headaches and was still having fits. Later he started to have Asthma attacks.

In 1969 he was hit by a car and badly injured. He was hospitalised and had to have a steel pin inserted in his leg from the hip to the knee.

Working at the Chequers Public House, a beer barrel caused him to have a bad fall in the cellar and working in a scrap yard he had his front teeth knocked out.

With even a few of Paul's problems, another person may have let them get him down, but they seemed to give him a stronger personality with a determination to live life to the full and even fuller.

He liked a drink and partying and the social life he led made him many friends.

Above all else he was a worker. He did manual work, barman in various pubs, in a scrap yard and does the arduous journey to and from London to work in the Albert Hall as a full time industrial cleaner, working five, six and even seven days a week when required.

He is a popular figure and has met many personalities who performed there, like Ronnie Scott, Eric Clapton and others.

He was never adverse to travel and holidayed in this country at various places and as far afield as Malta.

He became a firm supporter of a Rugby Club and was made their mascot. Although he attended twenty one matches, he never saw one of them. He was too busy doing other things.

He has been on the Committee of the Hainault Forest Community Centre for some years and holds membership card Number One that was bestowed on him by a past Chairman.

In the era of Teddy Boys he was one of them, a front runner and was often seen locally dressed up in his Ted's 'Uniform', Purple Jacket, with black velvet lapels, drainpipe trousers and to finish it off, black suede shoes with thick sponge soles 'Brothel Creepers' as they were termed.

They all met either in the Maypole in Fencepiece Road or the Black Raven in Aldgate, where dozens of 'Ted's' dressed up to the nine's packed the bars.

When Paul's Mum died in 2001 and his Dad in 2003, Paul had to move out of their house and was moved to a flat not far away, where he has built himself a 'Socialising Bar' where he can entertain his many friends.

In appreciation of his good work at the Albert Hall, a friend of his Alan Maffe, put his name forward to go to the Queens Garden Party and he attended it on the 19th July 2005, accompanied by Alan's wife Christine. His photograph shows him suitably attired for his trip to the Palace and he say's it was a great experience. A day he will always remember.

Another side to Paul is now evident, as he has been working hard since May 2005, trying to raise the sum of £1,500 towards sensual lighting

for the swimming pool at the Heybridge School for Handicapped Children, previously the 'Ethel Davis', it was a school that Paul once attended.
He never quite achieved the figure, but on the 31st January 2006 Paul, accompanied by Mick Willis the Manager of Hainault Forest Community Centre and his two friends, Alan and Christine Maffe, he presented the sum of £1,225 to the Headmaster and a photographer was there to record the event for the Ilford Recorder.
Sensual lighting that will be fitted into the ceiling above the pool and in its floor is a computerised system that generates light changes and sounds to stimulate the senses of the children using the pool. The Headmaster said 'The amount that Paul had contributed was the last part of the jig-saw puzzle that would allow the work to go ahead'.

Arthur S. for Paul 27.09.04 -31.01.06

Ilford Recorder 2.3.06

Grateful: Paul Chapman, left and Peter Bouldsbridge

Pupil's thank-you gift for old school

A Former pupil of a special needs school has given something back to the place that got him 'walking and talking'. Paul Chapman, 55, of The Lowe, Hainault, was at Ethel Davies School, Barley Lane, Goodmayes, as a youngster. The school has now merged with Hyleford to become Newbridge School, and is headed by Peter Bouldsbridge. Mr Chapman, who is a committee member of Hainault Forest Community Association, started his fundraising efforts modestly with a swear-jar in the bar at the club in Manford Way, Hainault. The jar soon filled up, not because everyone was foul-mouthed, but because people were so generous. It soon became an over-flowing bottle for people's loose change. Mick Willis, association chairman, said 'People put all their change in the jar and one of our brewers, Greene King, donated £200'. Further fundraising activities took place and Mr Chapman presented Mr Bouldsbridge with £1,225 in a ceremony at the school. He said 'I used to go there and I couldn't walk or talk when I started. I can now, so it can't be bad'. The money has allowed the school to press ahead with work to have sensory equipment installed in its swimming pool It is hoped the work will be finished within three months.

77

The Alfred's Head
By Jim Burns

The Alfred's Head the first new pub built on the Hainault Estate after the Second World War, was a regular meeting place for the local community and it holds many memories for Jim Burns who has been a regular there for more than thirty years.

He remembers that back then, Friday and Saturday nights were music nights and people would come from all around, arriving there in transit vans from as far afield as Basildon, Bethnal Green and different areas of the East End of London, giving it all a real Cockney flavour.

By 7pm, the customers would already be singing and dancing, their enjoyment going on until 'chucking out time' at 10.30pm. The pub was alive.

The regulars knew each other well and there was a real community spirit about the place. It was a sanctuary where people who had been separated by the war finally found each other and there were many joyful re-unions.

Back in the 50's and 60's it was an old style pub with its separate saloon and public bars and even a small jug and bottle bar. But like many pubs it underwent a transformation that, with extensions, increased the size of what was the saloon although the other bar still remains the same.

Now it seems the Alfred's may not be with us much longer, as a planning application to demolish the pub and build homes on the site has been lodged with the Council by a Housing Developer, although the brewery that owns it deny they have been approached to sell up.

Linda Berryman, who has worked as a barmaid for the last two years, said 'We still don't know what is happening and don't know what to tell our regulars who keep asking 'what the situation is'.

In the words of Jim 'It will be criminal if they close it down'.

It certainly doesn't look good for the Alfred's as two other local pubs have disappeared from the scene, the Hainault Oak that was on the corner of New North Road and Romford Road and the Badger that was in Manford Way.

The Oak, built in recent years on the site of its namesake, was one of the oldest pubs in the area that was demolished to make way for the new. Now the replacement has itself been demolished and a block of flats stands in its place. The Badger in Manford Way where Linda worked for twelve years has also gone and another block of flats has taken its place.

In Manor Road, Chigwell, a third pub once the Prince of Wales has also gone to make way for flats. At the end of the Second World War it was hit by a rocket, killing and injuring a number of customers, commemorated by a granite Memorial that stands on the site.

Unforgettable in Amber
by B.J.R

November 1949 will never be forgotten in our house, for it was the very day we packed our sparse belongings into a thirty hundred weight bull-nosed Morris Van and made our way off into the unknown, somewhere called Hainault. The whole operation took about two hours at a cost of £3 LSD. (half a week's earnings).

It was in the beginning, just a sea of molten yellow clay which stuck to everything and got everywhere.

We had two young sons and in no time at all they were camouflaged in the same colour; it was only when they blinked we found them.

This was the era when men lost the buttons off their flies and women were no longer considered tarts for wearing slacks. My wife had bought me a pair of light trousers with a big coarse zip like the jaws of a rampant crocodile. I have often wondered why, but did live to regret that.

The indigenous people were not over happy to see us, there were hardly any shops. Most groceries, milk and bread were delivered daily, either by horse and cart or motor van, at of course enhanced prices.

Time moved on. We got the mud off the boys and went to school, pavements were laid, street lights installed, (Gas lights in the Chigwell portion). Yet that did not detract from the amount of virgin clay left behind by the greedy contractors.

They had scraped clean the meadow land top soil off the whole area with a view to flogging it back to us when we all became garden conscious; some piles are still to be found around the area unused and unsold.

By far the most important condition of gaining access to a house on this Country Estate was based on the size of the family, bedrooms were allocated according to the children's sex.

This gave unlimited power to the minions employed in the rent office, one .or two of whom left a lot to be desired. Being no respecter of feigned authority I often fell foul of them,. A quick example, all front doors were painted in Council colours, of green or cream, I changed mine to blue and the rent collector nearly stood on his head, even threatening eviction, soon everyone was having a go.

No, these houses were not built for hero's, just sheer necessity, a year after the demob came the big baby boom,

I remember with a great amount of nostalgia the small self-contained prefabricated houses that were dotted all over the place, they lasted far longer than intended. The one little batch that I have fond memories of were on the playing fields on the corner of Elmbridge Road and Forest Road, there must have been over a hundred. Part of the site is now a traveller's camp.

In those days I was involved in the Hainault Industrial Estate and virtually became a member of their community, eventually joining their amateur drama group, they were called 'The Townsend Players', they had a small recreation hut complete with stage, it seated about forty to fifty people. The group were pretty self sufficient, in charge was a charming and experienced lovely lady named Mrs. Pfaff, she was a gentle taskmaster .

The Townsend Players 1956 - 1960

The successful production of many plays proved her popularity, I took one or two minor parts.

I had access to a large diesel van which was backed onto the stage door, when the sound effects of ship, car or airplane were called for, not withstanding the fact that the hall was a potential death trap from the fumes that filled it. Sometimes the audience could not see the stage and we took no notice of their coughing and sneezing.

The motto of the group- "The show must go on, even if it killed them".

All the props and flats for scenery were made and decorated by the local community.

The van doubled as a dressing room and a lot of fun and wisecracks arose from that.

There were a few shops, the only one to survive all those years is Bennets now situated in Manford Way Parade. Funny thing, the same old fashioned politeness and courtesy prevail in that shop.

Part of the old site has been dedicated to the Travellers, I believe the old hut is still there or has been renovated. We had darts and table tennis there, two of us decided to start a youth club and about twenty kids joined, but after about three weeks they all kept disappearing into the surrounding bushes, that stopped that enterprise.

One of the prime movers in that small society was called Jack Burrel, aged about thirty. He organised everything, sports, charabanc outings and different festivals. One of his more enterprising efforts was a bid to restore the old Fairlop Oak Legend. He planted an oak near to where the original was rumoured to be, advertising the fact as wide as possible in those days, it was not a roaring success as the weather killed it off.

When the main shopping centre was built everything changed, in former days if there was a glut or surplus of anything, someone would appear pushing a barrow with fruit and vegetables at about three half pence a pound and gradually the street callers like the coalman, cockles and winkles, baker, rag and bone, paraffin and general stores vans and of course the paper boys dissapeared...........now only the milkman re-mains, somehow or other we had more laughs in those times.

That little community has completely gone and gazing at the lush green sward, I ask myself, were these people just figments, I further imagine that in the fullness of time others will take their place.

This whole Estate of Hainault met and conquered the Battle of the Bulge, for it was the babies and young that were the original heart of this place, they now travel the world and fill some of the highest places in humanity and I have no doubt that when they pause to recall the memories set in amber, they will be as proud to call then selves..
'HAINAULTARIANS' as I am. A good pastime to look back, in Amber

Childhood Memories Of Living In Hainault
(up to early teens)
By Gillian Feldwhere

I was born in November 1951 in a two bedroom council owned house in Falconer Road, Hainault. My parents had moved there with my two brothers, Barry and Rodger from Bethnal Green.
Before my Sister was born in 1957, we moved to 33 Huntsman Road, Hainault, which was a three bedroom house. My Dad suffered from thrombosis after we moved there and I seem to remember him being in hospital for a very long time (6 months?) and me being shy of him when he came home. (I can't remember visiting him in hospital - not sure if children were allowed to at the time).
I can remember Jean being born downstairs at number 33 - in the dinning room which was used as a makeshift bedroom. Prior to this I can remember playing with a child called Sue Rose in our garden, who my Mum and Dad looked after whilst her Mum went to work. I still remain friends with Sue who now lives in Edinburgh.
Myself and Roger went to Coppice Junior School and I can remember walking to and from school every day. It was quite a long way as we were not allowed to take the short cut through Butchers Wood which was just across the top of Huntsman Road in New North Road. I can remember it being very foggy at times and not being able to see in front of you.
We played marbles on the "green" opposite our house. We also played run-outs, knock down ginger and used a rope to swing over the ditch at the bottom of the road near the factories. Because of the factories there were quite a lot of lorries using Huntsman Road as there was no width restriction at the bottom.
I seem to remember most children having bikes. I can remember cycling to Collier Row and going to a park there and the feeling of great achievement by making it to the top of Hog Hill without getting off the bike, this was before the top of the hill was 'shaved' off. We used to take our bikes over to Hainault Forest and race around a scrambling track in a copse there. My bike was a 'racer' with drop handlebars which was unusual for a girl!

I used to go bird nesting with Roger in Hainault Forest and we also used to sell golf balls to golfers which we had 'found' on Hainault Golf Course. We had to make sure that we weren't caught by the 'Parkies'. Our Mum used to work at Gainsborough Chocolate Factory on an evening shift and she used to put us to bed at 6pm before she went to work. It was still light and we could hear other children still playing outside! She used to bring chocolates home for us - soft centred- they were meant to be rejects!

Mum was always very good with money despite our Dad being a low earner. I can remember being the only one amongst my friends to have a fridge and fitted carpet! She always used to buy us a new Christmas and Easter outfit.

It was very cold in the house - there was no central heating. You could scratch patterns on the frost on the inside of the windows in the bedrooms in winter. There was a coal fire in the front room and paraffin fires in the kitchen and hall. Paraffin was delivered weekly or you used to get your cans filled at the shops at the 'top', a small parade of shops at the top of New North Road. You all had a bath once a week on a Sunday.

Dad used to play the piano in pubs to supplement the income. I can remember him playing in the Old Hainault Oak at the top of New North Road. In the lead up to Fireworks Night we used to collect pennies for the Guy outside this pub, as well as outside the factories on a Friday night (pay day). At Christmas we used to sing Christmas Carols at houses - private ones in the Chigwell area, and ask for money! None of the money went to Charity - it went into our pockets!

Hamilton Bakeries used to deliver bread and a fish man used to come round on Sundays. We used to have sweets from the ice cream man once a week - he used to stop at the corner of Huntsman and Falconer Road. I can remember buying Tizer and Cream Soda and taking the bottles back to get some money back.

I can remember listening to 'Family Favourites' on the radio on Sundays while we had lunch. We always used to have to listen to 'Sing Something Simple' on Sunday evenings, (Dad's choice!) On Saturday nights we watched 'Match of the Day' on television, (again Dad's choice!) My main recollection of television as a child was being frightened

'Quatermass' and peeping out from behind a cushion!
We used to play cards quite a lot with Dad and I used to play word
games with him. I went to the library regularly - where the Working
Man's Club is now. I read around four books a week!
I used to have to look after my Sister quite a lot and I remember having
to bribe her not to tell Mum and Dad about things that went on when
they were out! Once my friends and I shut her in one of the tall tin cupboards that came with the council house kitchen and it toppled over
with her in it!
Mum and Dad went to play bingo at East Ham when it became popular
and I can remember hearing that Kennedy had died one evening whilst
looking after Jean.
We weren't encouraged to have friends come into the house to play. I
can only remember Barry and Roger's friends coming in when Mum
and Dad were out. My friends used to stand on the doorstep to talk, or if
it was cold, just inside the hall.
Dad used to grow vegetables in the garden and also had an allotment. I
can remember having to cut the privet hedge outside the front and also
cut the grass out the back.
Relatives used to visit on Sunday afternoons. We were expected to be
on our best behaviour. We didn't have a car and Uncles used to take us
to Southend on Sundays in the summer, we saw relatives regularly. I
used to go with Dad on his motorbike to visit his sisters. Sometimes at
Christmas we had 'get togethers' with everyone singing and Dad playing the piano. Roger used to play the ukulele.
I can remember going to weddings of cousins regularly - I was a bridesmaid quite often as was Jean. Weddings were very much a family gathering!
We went on holidays to Clacton, Walton on Naze and Isle of Sheppey
and stayed in caravans or chalets. We had eels and mash in Walton on
Naze with liquor!
I can also remember once going to visit an Aunt who lived in Devon. I
also regularly went to stay with an Aunt and Uncle in Suffolk during
the summer holidays. They used to take us on trips to Ely Cathedral etc.
I can remember Barry going to work in London and Mum making him -
not us- a cooked breakfast everyday. Barry used to buy records and I

can remember him wearing a mohair suit with some sparkle like Perry Como on the television! He also used to have his collars for his shirts starched for work. Barry got married when he was 20. I was bridesmaid and Mum didn't allow me to wear stockings - I wore short socks!. Other things I remember about Barry when he was at school, was that he liked to ride horses and used to bunk off school. The truant man came round - Mum was not pleased!!

When I was about twelve I did a morning paper round before school, Kingswood Secondary Modern in Huntsman Road, for 10 shillings a week. The papers weighed a ton!

Youth Clubs were very popular and I remember playing table tennis, netball and dancing at Kingswood! Also went to Grange School sometimes. I also belonged to Dockland Settlement down at the Lowe. I was one of the children selected to meet Princess Margaret when she visited and was also chosen to be one of a group that went to see the premiere of a Beatles' film. I also went to the Church in Regarder Road and went on a camping holiday and attended a weekly social group. You used to have to take turns to help at the Sunday School.

Trolleybus
By John Bartholomew

Bus drivers and their families live a life separate from other people, shift work takes a terrible toll on any group. It disrupts the whole routine of daily life and all too often is the primary cause of the break up of young families.

The average bus driver is always tired, never quite recovering the rhythm of regular sleep and therefore inclined to be a bit touchy, especially about his job. The usual question, 'What shift you on today? was always boring, the job in itself being boring enough.

Old Ted used to tell me some tales when we were over the allotment at Hog Hill together, actually I think he enjoyed the job. He was working from a Trolleybus Garage on the corner of Ley Street and Perth Road, Ilford, Essex. At that time, in the early fifties, people depended more on public transport than they do today. The main services out of that garage were the No.691 trolley from Barkingside to Barking, a journey of some twenty seven minutes. Between that, in the rush hour, there were shorts and these only ran to Ilford Station, about thirteen minutes.

Every trolleybus had a conductor, complete with a rack of tickets and a punch bell that rang each time a ticket was bought.

On that particular route there were three main employers, Plesseys, Ilford Ltd and Howard Chemicals down Ilford Lane. According to the old chap, the object of the exercise was to get past the three as fast as possible when the workers were either going in or coming out. This was not always possible, for some of the Union Officials of the workers would take it on themselves to be at the bus stops at the proper time, watch in hand, eager to take the bus number if the driver tried to be too clever.

It is hardly credible in this day and age, that all that time ago the head-way between trolley buses from terminals was about two minutes in the rush hour and eight during the rest of the day. People in Ilford were lucky, at that time most were regarded as retired Civil Servants.

The London Passenger Transport Board had not long replaced the old LGOC The Omnibus Company. Ilfordians were accustomed to behaving as if they had in fact retired from the Colonial Service instead of the local Town Hall. Old Ted said they were in the habit of shooting out of a side turning brandishing a walking stick or an umbrella expecting the bus to stand on its nose for them. The terrible thing was, that if they did not get on and the person involved got the bus number, the poor old driver could be suspended, always without pay.

The great threat in those days was withholding a days pay and of course, most of the very ordinary working people momentarily in charge, were overcome by their power and revelled in it. There are a million tales of the crass injustice of men walking through ice and snow in the middle of the night to get to work on time, being told by some fatuous oaf, 'Too late, your bus has gone'. Ted told me of a chap on one occasion who replied humbly 'Please Sir, it hasn't gone yet, I asked him to wait a minute'. The answer was 'Who the bloody hell do you think you are, I'm running this outfit not you, you can bugger off home right now'. The hot headed youngster replied 'Cobblers to you, you miserable bastard to think we spent the war fighting for the likes of you, skulking behind that desk with flat feet, you can stick your job right up your jacksie' and then he stormed out of the door and never went back. Ted always seemed to be lucky, he very rarely lost a days pay, but then he had been at it a long time and knew all the answers. The bus fleets out of Ilford had been built for South Africa just prior to the second world war and at that time were the biggest ones in England, being eight foot wide and fitted with smoked glass windows, the conductor could talk to the driver quite easily. Over the years Ted had many conductors, one in particular made him laugh, he was a right clever bugger. There was always some sort of fiddle going on with regard to the fare monies collected, very rarely did either the driver or conductor pay for their tea out of their own pockets at each end of a journey. To compensate, the company employed a number of Spots, usually men dressed and acting as civilians to watch for fraud. The conductor that Ted found amusing was named Gio of Greek origin. The Spots knew for some months he had been fiddling, that means picking up used tickets and pretending to punch them anew, but as the bell went ding every time he re-issued one, it remained a mystery. One day he stumbled and fell and all was revealed. He had a false bell under his arm, so that every transaction sounded authentic. In a small depot such as Ilford, everyone new each other. In fact, when on the road the journey was so short, they all knew where each trolley should be at any given time. Those on the shorts would send their conductors to climb the advertising hoarding they parked behind to watch for the main trolley coming up from Barking. They would then slip in behind the one in front doing all the work. This was all part of the fun, everybody did it, some took it in good part, others didn't.

There was a terrific amount of rivalry between depots, sometimes if you were spare, you were sent on loan to another garage. You had been given time off to ride on and learn those foreign routes. Nobody ever did, so when the inevitable happened, it usually ended in chaos, for trolleys were confined to following the overhead electric cables which were interspersed with points called Frogs which changed the direction the arms travelled. If those Frogs were not activated at the right time the bus went one way and the booms every which way. In the fog and dark it was hard to capture them again with the eighteen foot bamboo pole supplied to all trolleys. For that purpose, it was so disappointing when there was not one available, for nine times out of ten, the bus was up the wrong road, even worse, when it was the last bus that night.

One other laughable thing about those bamboo poles, was when a six or even a seven stone woman conductor tried to reclaim them, she had to be rescued herself, the springs on the arms were so powerful. There was a terrific camaraderie in this small depot. The canteen was popular, it sported a snooker table and many times passengers were obliged to sit stewing outside the garage during change of crews for the last black in the game to be potted. Time was of the utmost. In Ilford Broadway was an Inspector named Johnson and he would hold a bus to the last thirty seconds, while at each terminal was a light duty man doing exactly the same thing. Ted still says that the idiot who wanted profit only by cutting the buses and increasing fares forty years ago, has been succeeded by a whole string of greater avaricious fools who know nothing of the transport service, driven to and fro in Government and Company cars, rarely setting foot on either a bus or maybe now and again, a train, deliberating on something they have not the slightest notion of. Pontificating purely from the stand point of shareholders, to the effect of having the proud and internationally admired London Passenger Transport Board reduced to the very same piratical practices it had risen from all those years ago. Most private enterprises end as victims to the curse of greed, for within the principal of every man for himself, that old devil will take the hindmost. Ted is indeed an unusual character, not usually given to long and deliberate speech, yet perhaps there maybe some truth in his deliberations. All this was brought about because I asked how life was treating him. So far, he has mentioned just the one route. In time no doubt, he will tell of the others. I am looking forward to that!

Hainault and Me

By Dan McMeekin

My first experience of the Hainault housing estate dates back, probably to 1953-4 when I was sixteen or so. At that time, I was serving an apprenticeship as a fitter and turner with a firm in Poplar. I would travel to work, either by trolleybus or by the underground, whichever seemed appropriate at the time. On this particular occasion, I was standing on Mile End station platform awaiting the District Line train marked Upminster, my stop was Becontree. My attention was drawn to a young lady, who similarly was awaiting a train, but in her case it was a Central Line train which would take her to Hainault.

A mutual attraction existed between us and as a result a date was fixed for an evening in Hainault. A number 62 bus served as my mode of transport for this exciting occasion. I soon learnt the time of the last bus which stopped at the corner of Regarder Road - it is a very long walk back to Becontree. My pioneering visit to New North Road, for that was where she lived, was closely monitored by my friends and subsequent to my report, (I remarked that the area was bursting with young ladies), the invasion was planned. Needless to say, many relationships were embarked upon. The venue in this case was the now defunct Grange Farm School in Manford Way, which at the time had a Youth Centre where youngsters could go and meet, even pursue further education. In our club in Becontree, I was a member of the boxing club and also attended typewriting and cookery classes, you find females in the latter two pursuits.

Why haven't the youngsters got these facilities today?

During the year or so of comings and goings to Hainault, prior to my entering the British Army to do my National Service 1955/57, a few relationships were struck up with different young ladies whose names I will not mention for obvious reasons. One in particular who was very special was unfortunately killed in a car accident. Some things are not to be. Who knows how life would have turned out had that not happened?

I have fond memories of using the local public houses, The Hainault Oak, The Old Maypole, The Maypole, but never the Alfred's Head. The Old Oak was a lovely friendly pub, the Old Maypole had entertainment on a Saturday evening with waiter service in the lounge. I remember a particular waiter who, having lost a hand, had a hook instead. The Maypole at Chigwell Row similarly had entertainment in the small long bar which was situated away from the main building at the rear. Smashing times! Some of the friends I have made since moving to Hainault remember the names of the characters that for instance played in the bands at these venues. Alas I do not.

Apart from my involvement in the gas conversion project in the early 70's, I had little reason to frequent the area until the late 90's, at which time I was employed by the local council as a gas and heating engineer which involved me very much in this area. I moved to the neck of the woods in 1995 and have been here ever since. In those eight years, I have seen the locale sink from a clean and tidy part of the suburbs to a scruffy dump. The folks who have lived here and brought their children up here must, in my opinion, be in total despair. Dumped cars and rubbish can be seen throughout the area with no apparent concern by some of the so-called local residents. I know I'm getting old and perhaps its a product of that situation that makes me feel the way I do in this respect, but it seems that some people do not possess any pride in their environment. I know some will say that when Queen Victoria died it all changed, but things certainly 'ain't what they used to be'. Food for thought I think, but who am I?

1st September 2003

A Short Poem
by Alan Hemmings

**I remember the days of '65
When we had fun and things were alive**

**Will I remember 2004 as not much fun
and really quite a bore?**

Doreen's Story

1955. Today I travelled from Carshalton to Chigwell for an interview with Mrs Percy Chandler. I had promised myself after leaving my job as a Nanny with the Brady family, that I would not put myself through the trauma of having to say goodbye again to a family I had grown to love as my own.

I had been a Nanny to Noel and Jill for ten years, now they were to be sent to Finishing Schools and no longer needed me! Saying goodbye to them and having to re-vamp my life had taken its toll of my emotions and again I had no roof over my head.

A hotel in Dagenham had been my home since I was seventeen and a half, during which time I had passed my Diploma and with the War not quite over I had to take a job where I could live in. Not having a house of my own this was essential, so luckily I had managed to get a job within a week of leaving training.

I was staying with my Grandfather when the job came up and the reason I was travelling from Carshalton was that I was living in the Nurses Home at Carshalton Hospital. I wanted to gain extra experience of children with Cerebral Palsy, as I thought I might like to become a Nanny to one such child.

Queen Mary's at Carshalton had allowed part of their Polio ward to be used for the purpose of training Nurses or future Nannies to become competent with such children. Doctor Collins was in charge of the ward.

I would point out that Doctor Collins was the Doctor Cole in the film 'My Left Foot'. The story of a young boy with Cerebral Palsy (Christy Brown) who taught himself to write with a pen held between the toes of his left foot. While I was there, I was privileged to meet this young boy who was about fourteen years old at the time.

He was very impressive to watch I can assure you and I loved every moment of my job on the ward, although I had to lose my status as a Nanny and become a Ward Orderly. I didn't regret this one jot and I had such a deep respect for these young people, struggling to keep their limbs still, long enough to eat or talk.

So you ask what am I doing travelling to Chigwell to have an interview as a Nanny? I was asking myself that same question as I came into Woodford Bridge on the number 25 bus from Victoria.

The Chandlers lived in a house called 'Inglenook' in Stradbrooke Drive three doors from Bobby Moore. At that time, 1955, the Brady's were friends with the Chandlers and found they needed a Nanny for their two children Anne and Bobby.

Mrs Chandler had asked Mrs Brady if her Nanny would be interested and I got a phone call at the hospital, and here I am at 'Inglenook' ringing their doorbell. Within a month, I became their Nanny and moved into a bedroom over their garage.

As soon as I got settled I took the children down to the village called Woodford Bridge. I loved it immediately, the lovely smell of hot baked bread in the village bakery, the row of shops sold everything imaginable. The Cafe, where after we had shopped I took the children in for a hot chocolate and a plate of house-made pastries.

On our way back to 'Inglenook', we would pass the village pond and play ball on the grass beside it. How the bells in the beautiful Village Church would ring out at the weekends, ringing out wedding chimes and all around a feeling of peace you would find hard to explain.

On other days when there was no school, we would catch the number 25 bus by the pub and go all the way to Victoria. The children loved those bus rides, it made such a change from riding in the Bentley or Mrs Chandler's MG Sports which they found boring as they just took them from A to B, whereas on the bus they could enjoy their surroundings, sitting in the front seat on the upper deck. I missed the life of the busy hospital and all the new friends I had made, but all in all I never regretted going back into the world of the Nanny.

There were three of us, Claire, Nanny to Bobby Moore's children, Robert and Dean. Then Irish Mary in the big house on the corner of Manor Road, Nanny to the Monnas' children, Victor and Elise. Mrs Monnas was an ex-Cochran girl. She married Percy Chandler's brother Robert. Then of course there was myself.

What times we had together, parties in each other's houses, three Nannies and six children. Wonderful Days.

Then along came Bill, but that's another story. See You!

Hainault Cubs and Scouts
By Paul Silverman

In 1962 my universe was enlarged on a scale I could not imagine at the time. There were several Scout groups dotted around the Hainault estate - ones that I recall are the 5th Ilford North by Hainault Station and the 9/10th Ilford North, at first two separate groups, but later combined into the 19th Ilford North based behind the Alfred's Head. There may have been more but I can't remember now. In my latter teenage years, the Hainault Venture Scouts were able to recruit Scouts from the 5th, 19th and 12th Ilford North.

The 12th Ilford North became central to my life. Already at age nine, friends at school were Cubs in that pack. The Scout group was based in a hut behind St Paul's Church in Burrow Road. I enrolled as a Wolf Cub and left as an Assistant Cub Leader in the early 1980's when pressure of work and the disability grew too much to cope with loud and lively children. As a Cub, a Scout, Venture Scout and then an Assistant Cub Leader, I learned about camping, knots and first aid, but also about friends. Over the years we went camping at Hargreaves (down Hainault Road) and, as we grew older, on to various other places around the country. I was fortunate in becoming a Cub Instructor while a young teenager as it helped me develop other skills and go to places with both Cubs and Scouts. The Scout group, being attached to the church (and having Peter Garner, the then Vicar at St Paul's, as group Scout Leader for a while) was also affiliated at the time to the Church Army. This was not an extremist Christian organisation, rather it meant that we had access for a week each summer to a campsite at Seasalter in Kent. I went there first as a Cub aged about nine and later a few times as a helper. A group of the Scouts and Guides at St Paul's would go along, sleep in caravans while the Cubs were in huts and generally help out. Going swimming in the chilly waters, organising games and helping to teach were as routine as the evening campfires and everyone would have a laugh before the Cubs went off to their huts to sleep.

21/06/04

Gone and Almost Forgotten
By A Salton

We moved here in 1957 when the roads were still pink concrete, not black asphalt as is now predominant. Our house in Manford Cross was massive compared with the three small rooms my family, a wife and two young children, had left behind in Bow, East London.

Our expenses were higher, rent was eleven shillings a week in Bow, now it was two pounds here in Hainault. I cycled to work in London, now there were fares to find between Hainault and Borough Underground Station that I remember as being three and sixpence a day, old money. Whatever it was, it put a considerable strain on our finances. There were compensations with the fresher air and the forest near at hand where we could all wander and play at weekends and there were other things to see and places to go to that were all near at hand.

There were places around that were part and parcel of Hainault, but have all disappeared over the years as the area has progressed and the following changes are what I can remember having taken place in the 47 years we have lived here.

* The pre-fabs that were located along Manford Way, New North Road and Forest Road.

*The old cottage in New North Road demolished to make way for new housing.

*The picturesque cottage on Hog Hill with its large informal garden, once the site of Hog Hill House. Demolished in the late 50's early 60's, the site now back to nature with its mass of tangled brambles that is now a nature reserve.

*The Synagogue that was once in Huntsman's Road where houses now stand.

*The small holding on reservoir land in New North Road where the holder kept ducks and chickens and a large allotment. He left it when it was taken over by the British Legion who built a new hall on the site. In the late 90's they left it and the building was turned into a Social Club which itself closed down in 2002 and the building was due to be demolished, but on the 21st September 2004 it was almost destroyed by a fire.

*The old barn at Hainault Forest that was once the Tearoom for park visitors, but is now storage space for their maintenance vehicles.

* The Old Hainault Oak Pub was a little old country pub with cottages alongside it until back in the 60's they were all demolished and a trendy new pub was built in its place and new housing built on where the cottages used to be. The Hainault Oak has now been demolished and at this moment, 26th September 2004, a block of flats are being built in its place.

* The garage that was on the corner of Tunstall Road, Manford Way was a proper little country type garage for repairs and petrol, that was demolished to make way for a petrol station, that in its turn closed down, everything ripped out and a block of flats built on the site.

*Butcher's Wood as it was called. A strip of the old Hainault Forest that ran between New North Road and Manford Way became the site for the flats that are now at Yellow Pine Way.

*The Youth Club in Manford Way originally paid for by local residents. Opened by Princess Margaret under the auspices of the South Poplar Youth Club, but eventually ran into problems and was disused, until the Council suddenly had it demolished and a sheltered accommodation block was built in its place.

* Hainault High School was once called Kingswood.

*The Catholic School that was in Manford Way was demolished and new housing built there.

* A brand new public house 'The Badger' was built in Manford Way back in the 70's, then two years ago it was closed and has since been demolished and at the moment a block of flats is being built there.

26.09.2004

Hainault. Where's That?
ASA. 12.12.05

Married in 1952 my wife Bet and myself thought we were fortunate in getting three rooms upstairs in a house where I was born in Bow. However, the woman downstairs was a stroppy ex Land Army Girl who complained and moaned about everything we did. She was worse when our daughter was born a year later and we were involved in regular rows with her. So what should have been a happy time was made miserable. Our son was born in 1955, which never improved the situation. As I was at work most of the time, Bet suffered more than I did.

We were overjoyed when we had a letter from the Greater London Council in 1956 telling us that our house was to be cleared away under 'slum clearance' and would we let them know where we would like to go?

We had no idea really, but the area that was on everyone's lips as the up and coming place to live with a large garden to go with the house was Debden. So that's where we put down.

Some weeks later we received another letter advising that a house had been allocated to us at the address Manford Cross, Chigwell and we were to pick the keys up from the rents office in Manford Way.

We'd never ever heard of either Hainault or Chigwell, but making enquiries, we found they were stations on the Central Line, so on the following Saturday the four of us made our way to Mile End Underground Station and booked our tickets to Chigwell.

Arriving there we enquired of the ticket collector (they were about then) the whereabouts of Manford Way, he said 'Not here, you need to go to Grange Hill', so back on the platform we went and caught a train to Grange Hill where another ticket collector directed us out of the station to Manford Way, the first on the right.

The day was lovely, the sun was shining and the greenery of the fields and tree's opposite the station showed off in its light. Walking into Manford Way after the years in the East End of London was all a delight to the eye.

The houses neat and clean with colourful front gardens, the pavements unspoiled and with the grassy strip running between it and the clean pink concrete road, it was a complete contrast to the streets we had left at Mile End.

Making our way down the road passing the pre-fabs that were on either side, we called into the Rents Office collected the keys to the house and followed the directions. 'Straight down the road until you come to the main road, The Lowe (what a surprise for a main road that was) carry straight on and Manford Cross is the next turning on the left.

Before long we were turning the key in the door and exploring the house that with its huge living room and space made our three pokey rooms back in Bow minuscule.

The garden was a disappointment, it wasn't very big and of a peculiar shape and layout, but the house won and we decided to accept it and made our way back to the Rents Office to confirm it.

After making enquiries of people we met on the way back, we found out Hainault Station was nearest and caught a bus to there. That was the first of our many journey's we would make in the future from Hainault to London and back again.

We received the date, April 1957, when we could take over the house and were advised the Greater London Council would allow us seventy pounds as moving expenses.

Arrangements were made with removal men (two men and a medium sized van) to take our belongings to Hainault, charging us an amount that fitted in with our allowance.

Even though we only had three small rooms, as Bet found out because the packing of everything fell on her shoulders as I was working, that it was a big headache getting what we had packed into tea chests that were available then and generally used for removals, but we were ready for our big move by the due date.

The removal van was just about big enough to take what we had and when everything was packed in, it was so overloaded that bits stuck out at the back, but as we were going we were so pleased to leave our downstairs neighbours behind. We had no worries about it all getting there.

When our furniture and other bits were unloaded at the Cross, the house swallowed them up. The carpet that had covered almost the entire floor in the old house now just covered up a portion in front of the fireplace of the cold brown asphalt floor.

We had space to move around in and it was so obvious as my son at one year old wasn't walking because of the restricted place we had left, but after just a week or so in the new place he was running around.

It was a 'swings and roundabouts' situation as apart from the good things about our move, we had money problems to overcome as we were only paying eleven shillings a week rent for the three rooms in the old house, now this one required two pounds ten shillings. Then there was my fare to work that for me was near the Borough Underground Station.

We had hard winters in the early years. The worst was in 1963-4 when we had the same snow on the ground for ten weeks before it eventually melted away. On the first morning after it fell the buses weren't running and with the steady stream of workers walking to Hainault Underground Station, it looked like a scene out of 'The retreat from Moscow'. In the winter the house was so cold, the floor was concrete with an inch of hard brown asphalt over it and the plastic flooring we had would curl up at the edges with the cold and the only place we could sit in the living room was directly in front of the fire where we scorched on the front and froze on our back.

This only changed when some years later we bought a stove an 'Esse Autovector' that put all the heat of the fire into the room and we were able to sit further away from it.

Of course then it was solid fuel and we burnt Coalite. Fuel was also in short supply at the time and Bet, my wife, made regular trips to the Coal Merchants that used to be in Barkingside by the Underground Station to chase up late deliveries and it was stored in a concrete bunker in the back garden.

Whatever type of solid fuel fire one had, they all had to be started off with newspaper and wood and it wasn't always as simple as it sounds, because fires like everything else so it seems can be a bit temperamental and wouldn't want to catch.

Different tricks were used to draw the fire into life if it was obstinate, like holding a sheet of newspaper over the fireplace opening, which would cause a draught to go in underneath the fire concentrating the oxygen supply when the fire would really roar into life until one had to be careful that the newspaper didn't burst into flames as it so often did with the heat.

The real change came about when we had gas central heating installed some 20 years ago and the house became comfortably warm for the first time. It was worth all the mess and upheaval we had to go through to have it done.

48 years have rolled by and so much has happened to Hainault in that time, just like many other places we seem to suffer over the shortage of money, with cracked uneven pavements patched up where contractors channel out pavements and roads to lay their high tech cables all over and uneven black tarmac reigns supreme as an apparent temporary/permanent modern filling.

Even the roads have succumbed and black tarmac is the new pink as they say nowadays. Rubbish seems to be the order of the day, although the sweeper does a good job removing it from our local shopping area. However, the biggest change that has come about is with the population. The influx of Ethnic minorities has begun to turn Hainault into a truly Cosmopolitan area.

ASA. 12.12.05

The Twilight Shift
By Marion Osborn

In the olden days, before child care facilities were widely available, the only way young mums could earn money was to work evenings, whilst their husbands looked after the children. To fill this niche, some local factories operated twilight shifts, which usually were six until ten in the evening, Plesseys, Magnavox, Ever Ready, Dicky Birds, to name but a few - all long since defunct. Because they usually operated these shifts when they were busy, or a particularly urgent order had come in, the jobs were, by their very nature, temporary, and quite difficult to come by.

As a hard up new mum, I applied for, and got, a job at Dicky Birds ice cream factory. It was with some trepidation that I went there, for as an ex pen-pusher I had no experience whatsoever of factory work and assembly line work was absolutely unknown to me. Everybody had one specific job to do, as items jostled along on the moving conveyor belt. If you weren't quick enough, you found yourself running alongside the belt, endeavouring to complete your task before it reached the next operator. I was very much afraid of being a duck out of water, and so it proved, for the first obstacle I came up against was the dreaded turban. This was compulsory wear for hygienic reasons. I hadn't a clue of how to put it on and as a consequence it was always slipping down and hanging in my eyes. All the other girls managed to tie theirs most becomingly and I knew they were all poking fun at me.

One evening, when I was struggling to put it on, one of the girls said 'Give it here, I'll show you how to fix it properly'. With a few twists of her deft fingers, it was done. I was eternally grateful to her, but most importantly, I was in with the in-crowd. For when it became known that Doris had taken me under her wing, I was accepted and became the baby of the group as most of the women were nearly twice my age.

As we were laid off from one firm, word went round of the next place that needed workers and we all went together to get the jobs. So, over the years I became a proficient ice cream and battery packer, an expert electronics assembly line worker, stuffed Xmas crackers and learned to use a soldering iron.

Most firms operated a piecework scheme, whereby if you exceeded a fixed target you got extra money. The only problem was that the figure to beat was based on the fastest worker there and if you did manage to equal it, they immediately upped the target. But I must admit it was an excellent way to get maximum effort out of the workers, because everybody tried to obtain that elusive bonus.

£3 a week doesn't sound much now, it wasn't much then!, but it gave you a bit of money that you could call your own to spend on the little extras that your partner's money couldn't stretch to. We called them husbands then, but it seems such an outmoded term now! You had to clock in and clock out and if you were a minute late you lost a quarter of an hour's pay. I well remember some of the girls moaning about the poor wages. It got to the ears of the management and we were all assembled for a meeting.

'Rumours are rife that some of you aren't satisfied with the pay. If so, they can leave now. For everyone of you, we've got two waiting outside the gates for your job'.

Needless to say, nobody moved. Problem sorted!

When we finished work at the stroke of ten, we all rushed to the clocking out machine and joined the queue. Then we dashed outside the factory gates, only to invariably see our ten o'clock bus go sailing past. Some, never to be forgotten, kind drivers used to wait for us and got a resounding cheer from us as we boarded.

The laughs and the jokes we shared and the characters and the courage of those women are with me still after all these years. They were the salt of the earth and wonderful with it. The names of my colleagues come jostling to the forefront of my mind.

Daisy always wore these awful old fashioned brown clodhopper boots, which must have originally been her farm worker grandmother's. Summer or winter she always had them on. One evening, whilst we were packing ice lollies on the conveyor belt, she was ribbing me about the way I was dressed in a mini skirt. I never answered, just smiled and carried on working, but one of the young day workers who was doing a spot of overtime, defended me 'At least she's modern'. 'Modern? what d'you mean modern? I'm modern!' Daisy was quite indignant. As we bent to our task to hide our grins, the day worker whispered to me

'Dig those crazy boots!'
Jessie had ten children - yes ten! 'Beats me how you find the time to do evening work' I said. 'Organisation' she replied. 'The kids all have their jobs to do and the big ones look after the little ones. Truth be known, I probably don't work as hard as you do with your one'. Somehow I couldn't quite believe her.

Another of the girls was beautiful, Belinda, with her five children. She always looked so terribly sad. One day she told me why. She'd got herself pregnant by another man and her husband had taken her back on the condition that she gave the baby up for adoption when it was born. She'd agreed to his terms, but the baby turned out to be twins and now she couldn't forgive herself for what she'd done. The five she had couldn't compensate for the guilt she felt at giving up those twins.

Then there was Bridget. Dear daft as a brush Bridget. Pregnant with her fourth child, she didn't want management to know, in case they laid her off. So she wore a big loose coat and got all of us to crowd round her, back and front, as she entered and left the factory. Her pregnancy seemed to go on forever and the baby she told us was due in February was actually born in April, and that was what she named her. 'I got muddled up with my dates' she giggled.

Snooty Pam, who bragged her kids were so well behaved that she could leave them sitting at the table and go to Ilford and they'd still be sitting there when she got back. She said she didn't need the money, she just went to work to buy herself nice underwear. Just the opposite, was poor downtrodden Joan, who used to take two unpaid weeks off at Christmas so that she could deliver the Christmas post. There she'd be in all weathers, tramping the streets with her pram piled high with letters, because she said the pay was better.

I remember those as happy days. The camaraderie was brilliant and you were never long enough at one firm to get bored. I worked like this for five years until my son went to school, when I got a proper job as a trainee dental nurse. But that's another story.........

An Unforgettable Adventure - Ten Years On
By Beryl Risbridger

The Wednesday morning meeting of the Hainault Writers had begun perfectly normally. Little did I know then it was to be the start of one of the most nerve-racking, unforgettable times of my life.

Our Tutor, Richard, breezed in as usual. After a few generalities, he said he had been approached by the Head Teacher of Hainault High School, asking whether we would be prepared to write about our varied experiences from 1939 to 1945 as a project for the GCE exam for the following year, which would then be the 50th Anniversary of the end of the War.

We discussed the suggestion and decided that we would be quite willing to have a shot at it. We had in the Group several Evacuees and men who had served in the Armed Forces, so the project was started. Each week we would read out our own experiences; some funny and others that brought a lump to the throat and tears to the eyes.

One Wednesday, Richard announced that we were to have a couple of visitors to discuss the project and so Harriet and Claire entered our lives. Harriet was a quiet, very talented musician and Claire, who was equally talented, somewhat louder American who was to be employed to turn our various reminiscences into a script. 'That's alright' we thought, until the crunch came when Claire asked who would like to take an active part in it. One or two of our Members had been involved in Amateur Dramatics in the past and were quite happy to 'sign up'. Just the thought of it filled me with horror, so I volunteered to make the tea! I should add that almost ten years on I am still doing it!

The next step was to meet the pupils who would be involved. So we made our way to the theatre at the school. We were greeted with the noisiest, ill mannered group we had ever encountered. How we didn't turn tail then I'll never understand! We discovered later that when our group of 'oldies' arrived, the kids took one look at us and decided that we would do nothing but moan at them! How wrong we both were! Although we had some sticky moments during the following months, we formed genuine affections and mutual respect.

Gradually our various ramblings began to take shape into a reasonable script. Harriet fashioned some of our poems into lyrics and put them to music. Teresa and I were asked to write one bringing in when the Yanks came over. It was quite fun and became a showpiece for four of the girls, preparing to go out on a date, singing 'I'm going out tonight, I'm going out with a Yank' and they always enjoyed it. Part of this eventually became the title of the show - 'Gas Mask On My Shoulder'. Our men were cajoled into performing a funny song about, of all things, Spam! Unless you had been in the War, the real significance of the arrival of Spam would probably be lost on you.

Over the following months and, much to our amazement, the script became moulded into an almost credible show, mainly thanks to Claire, who was a very pushy, persuasive Yank (her words, not mine!). Seriously though, we had become very fond of both of them.

Then a terrible blow fell when Teresa was diagnosed with a serious illness and had to go into hospital for an immediate operation. She was our most enthusiastic Amateur Dramatic person and was really looking forward to taking a major active part in the play. What were we to do? The only other person to take over was me and Claire's 'persuasion' really took off! Either I took over or the whole thing would collapse. So what could I do, but agree. I was petrified. I had no acting ability whatsoever; couldn't project my voice and could only see me ruining the whole production.

Anyway, we plodded on and the day of the first performance loomed ever closer. We did one at the Community Centre which went quite well, except the sound system was inadequate. There was another in the school hall with an audience of three hundred plus pupils. I felt sorry for them as I imagined they would be so bored but, much to my amazement, they appeared to thoroughly enjoy it and even joined in with the Wartime songs at the end that we had sung all those years ago, at roundabout their age. There was a disastrous performance one afternoon in the school's theatre to a totally unresponsive audience, in particular one Teacher who obviously did not want to be there and sat the whole time with his arms folded and a completely unexpressive look on his face. This put a real downer on us all. The Local Authority laid on a performance at the Town Hall for pensioners, providing them with transport, tea and cakes, which was probably an inducement for them to come, as it was a freebie It was such a hot day and the sun poured in from the glass roof. There was a minor hiccup when one of the adult leads went walkabout, but was found just in time in a local pub! The pensioners seemed to really enjoy this trip back in time and filled the rafters with the Wartime songs at the end.

Then there were to be two performances at the Barbican. This time our errant walkabout performer was guarded absolutely everywhere he went! Had he disappeared at the Barbican, he'd never have been found! The early performance attracted quite a few people, in particular a young family who sat right in the front. The performance had hardly begun when they all got up and walked away. What a blow to our confidence; surely it wasn't that bad? As it happened they returned for the second performance and were thoroughly enthusiastic. It appeared that they had tickets for something else and that was why they had to leave. The second performance was one of our best, thankfully, and appeared to be really enjoyed by the audience of quite a few hundred.

The final performance was on May 8th, exactly 50 years to the day from VE day in 1945. It was to be in the Veterans Tent in Hyde Park. We boarded the coach at Hainault and were dropped outside the park. We were given a pass with 'Artist' on it, which we had to wear and this enabled us to come and go any time.

We were the last act of the day. The act supposed to be before us hadn't turned up, so we were brought forward. Richard had warmed up the large crowd with his marvellous piano playing and we were about to start, when lo and behold the latecomers arrived and we had to stop. What an anti-climax! This put everything behind time and when eventually we did begin, a wretched Tannoy kept blaring out all over the park, including the Veterans Tent, insisting that everywhere had to be cleared by 5.30pm so that the evening audience for the pop concert would be able to come in. The microphones weren't working and what with the Tannoy's noise our youngsters, in particular, were becoming agitated and ready to call it a day. Somehow we persuaded them to carry on, despite all the problems. The audience were really marvellous and stayed with us to the end.

The finish was something I'll never forget. When Richard played his heart out with the Wartime medley, the audience were on their feet, singing their socks off and eventually forming an enormous chain, dancing the Conga! They just didn't want us to go, but we had no choice as the coaches were only allocated a specific time. I was very proud that one of my poems had been put to music by Harriet and was the finale. I had called it 'We Survived' which was exactly what we had done.

It was a day that I will never, ever forget, full of smiles, tears and Patriotism welling up in everyone. We felt so proud to be British and lucky enough to have lived through a terrible War and an overwhelming sadness for those who hadn't made it.

January 2005

Letter To Jack Re Gas Mask

HAINAULT
17th December 1994

Dear Jack

Eric and I so enjoyed the recent production of 'Gas Mask On My Shoulder', that I am writing to you to ask you to pass on our appreciation to all those involved - yourself included! It was really great to see the spirit which existed between the different age groups.

Actually it brought back one of my own 'Wartime' memories. I lived in Leyton at the time and I was aged about five. It was night time, I was fast asleep in bed. A 'Rocket' landed about a hundred yards further down our road, there was a tremendous blast. Amongst other damage, the wall immediately behind my bed practically collapsed - all the bricks came hurtling down on the pillows and bed and yet, amazingly, I was unhurt. I can remember my mother rushed up from downstairs in an absolute panic. I hadn't thought about this for years - it was your production that brought it to mind again.

Anyhow, the main purpose of this letter is to ask you to express our thanks to all involved in the production - it was great.

Yours sincerely

Pat Gleave

A

COMMUNITY ARTS

PROJECT

PRODUCTION

GAS MASK ON MY SHOULDER

Redbridge
LONDON BOROUGH

Spare Tyre
Theatre
Company

'Gas Mask' The Cast in the Veteran's tent for the
V.E. Celebrations in Hyde Park. 1995

At rehearsals. 1995

Getting Around Hainault
By Paul Silverman

Aged eleven I was given a bike to help me get around the estate and that did a sterling service until I learned to drive later on. During my teenage years I was able to ride from one end of the estate to the other without any difficulty. These were full of experiences and the bicycle helped me reach the shops and wander around the estate with friends as well as enabling me to go further. I would leave it at Hainault Station, catch the Tube into London and go to places with family and friends. That bike was a lifesaver as my disability began making my life harder from the age of about ten.

The next step, learning to drive a car, added new horizons to my life. I first learned to drive one of those three wheeled invalid cars. The law stated that no passengers were allowed so a man from the BSM came along and showed me the controls and then told me to drive down Arrowsmith Road. For the few lessons he would run behind me until I couldn't see him any more and then I would stop! Thankfully this worked and I didn't hit anything or anyone with him dashing along behind. People in Arrowsmith Road came out to watch and frankly it was a farce. I had no problems and kept the tiny three wheeler under control and then stopped. He came wheezing along and lit a fag when he reached me! After a couple of lessons we moved on to lessons where he told me what to do at speed.... and then followed or led the way in his car. It was as well that I had good nerves at that age. The driving test for that was like a motorcycle. The examiner told me what he wanted and stood on a corner where he could see me. I passed that driving test aged seventeen and about four years later I learned to drive an ordinary automatic in which I could seat an instructor and examiner. In later years these became as important as my legs for getting around. Unfortunately traffic grew in Hainault as it did everywhere else and the issue became more one of parking.

21-06-04.

Going To School In Braeside in 2004
By Ysanne Harding (aged 15)

Braeside is situated on the edge of Essex, in Buckhurst Hill. Braeside is surrounded by lush green trees. The back of the school overlooks a beautiful garden, which is home to lots of kinds of wildlife. When driving from London to Essex the temperature drops slightly and as you get further into Essex the houses get bigger and there is a lot of open space. Braeside is a large Victorian house that has a very detailed history. It still contains historic features such as fireplaces, doorplates, sash windows and a bell tower overlooking the road.

Braeside has managed to keep the unique Victorian features yet adapt to the use of technology and the forever growing list of different kinds of subjects. Braeside has recently set up a network of laptops which are a great advantage to Business Studies, a new subject we study. Braeside pupils also enjoy PSHE, Careers and Citizenship lessons, which are enhanced with new technology such as overhead projectors and televisions. The Science Labs and Art and Drama Rooms are all new additions to the building. Although they are built for modern purposes they have been built to fit in with the Victorian style house.

A big aspect of school life is the houses. Braeside has four houses that are all named after famous women. They are called: Mason, Nightingale, Fry and Bronte.

Throughout the year we compete for prizes. We hold debate competitions in which the pupils choose the topics. We also take part in sports events such as rounder's, Carols, play competitions at Christmas and the Conduct Cup. Having houses is a fantastic opportunity to work as a team with new people from every year. Braeside is a close unique school where everyone knows everyone.

Did Aliens Visit Hainault?
By A Salton

It was 23.45 on the 31st May 1988. I'd been working late in London and was in my car driving home. There was no traffic about as I drove down Manor Road past Grange Hill Underground Station and turned into Manford Way where an amazing sight got my attention.

Before my eyes over the roof of one of the houses in front of me was what is termed an Unidentified Flying Object, although this object wasn't flying, it was just hanging there and although it seemed to be above the house, it was actually way over in the distance.

Its length was about two thirds of the length of the roof, its shape an elongated oval. Almost the proverbial Cigar Shape, its curved surface seemed to be made of a dull silvery material lit up by lemon coloured lighting.

Its shape was surrounded by a corona of light and a bright light as though from a searchlight without a beam, lit up heavy black clouds above it and although I only saw the side view, I was of the impression it wasn't a tubular shape, but there was so much more of it beyond the curved side I was viewing. Not realising how Manford Way swept round in a big curve, I continued along the road thinking I might get a better view of the craft further down the road, but it wasn't to be.

As I approached the sharpest part of the bend of Manford Way by Parkes Road, there were maisonettes that had a big box shaped tank room on top and just as though someone had a left a skylight open on it, a powerful beam of light was shining into the air, the same light I'd seen above the UFO. In the last year or so, the roof has been changed to a different shape.

As I got near to the shops, high in the sky was a large orange coloured wedge shape moving at a fantastic speed in a southerly direction, the thick end of the wedge in the front.

Later on I checked the positions where I made the sightings against a map and estimated that the UFO could have been over the lake in Hainault Forest.

I regret to this day not stopping my car and getting out to have a good look while I had that sight of it. But one thing is for sure, whoever, or whatever it was, they certainly never made any attempt to conceal the fact they were there. I would be interested to know whether anyone else would have had the same sighting.

07.07.04

Hainault Forest - Escape From The City
By Jo Baker

As soon as the car doors open they dash off, running and hiding alongside the parallel ridges, pretending to be soldiers.

The grass stretches down to a lake and trees in front of us. Behind lies the city, even Canary Wharf is visible, but the urban landscape fades into the haze. We too run down towards the lake, caught up in the exhilaration of so much green space.

The children stop and stare at a gaggle of Canadian Geese, standing on the lake's shore. The geese stare back, immobile, a forest of long straight necks, legs and mottled wings. Suddenly one launches into the water. The rest splash in after, like water lemmings on a mission.

We follow the yellow-stone road as it winds in towards the trees. The children run ahead, but we relax, knowing there are no cars to run them down here.

A yellow-green bird lands from its bobbing flight in the grass a little way ahead. I call to the children to be quiet, creep closer and have a look. It takes a while, but eventually they see its red-capped head and bright beak sticking out of the grass - a green woodpecker.

Then they're running off down the track into the trees, soldiers again. There's plenty of cover and sticks for guns. We too jump ditches, or cross them on rickety logs. The sun filters through the leaves, lighting dappled glimpses of forgotten times.

We're all explorers now - centuries away from the city. A squirrel freezes, its little black eyes fixed on us, then dashes across last year's dry leaf-litter and spirals up a tree until he's lost in the branches. The canopy shakes above us as he lands on twigs just strong enough to take his weight. Then he's gone again, racing and leaping across his vast playground.

They're stealthy huntsmen now with bows and arrows, moving silently (or silently for them). Now we're the hunters and they try to hide, but parents' eyes never quite lose them. 'Hey look at this!'

He's found a carved post with a silver moon nailed onto it. Forest art. Intrigued, we look for more strange artefacts from a lost civilisation. A bench, no, a swaddled face- carved from a tree trunk. The forest is full of surprises. Time to go and part from staffs' guns and bows. They lay them down, reluctantly, at the edge of the forest already dreaming of next time.

Bat Walk At Fairlop Waters
By Hazel Dongworth

October red sun
low over lake,
waterbird calls,
signals to roost.
Twilight track,
through tree-lined gloom,
sky, silhouette-clear,
dusk, falling fast.

Owl-cry dark,
slow black wings
quick bat loops
as prey mobs hunter.
Insect-warm night,
volley of low passes,
busy streaks and trails....
cold, still blackness.

Torch-trudge back,
ink-thick air,
star-flicks, moonrise,
alien street lamps.
Light polluted tidiness,
mature tree-loss,
green islands marooned
in a concrete and tarmac sea.

My Visit To Hainault Country Park
By Ivy Brown

Sitting in the country park
Watching the cloudless sky
Reflect its colour on the lake
Was pleasing to the eye

The water was so very calm
The surrounding trees so green
And ducks swimming peacefully
Completed the lovely scene

My attention was diverted
When along the footpath came
A couple with their puppy dog
Who wished to play a game

He rushed up and touched my leg
But not too aggressively
And when I said 'Hello my friend'
He seemed to smile at me

His owners too were smiling
As they called their pet away
Somehow I knew this would be
A very happy day

Then across the lake swam lots of geese
Of the Canadian kind
Once on dry land they searched around
To see what they could find

I found them most amusing
Quite a sight to see
But I must say I was hoping
They wouldn't come near me

Not that I'm suggesting
They would do me any harm
But just in case I went away
And visited the farm

There were birds of prey, a pig, some goats
But sadly not much more
Certainly not such a variety
As when I went before

Although that seemed a pity
The visit was worthwhile
For all the creatures that were there
Entertained in style

So if you like the countryside
Take a tip from me
Help the Hainault Forest Country Park
Celebrate its centenary

Spring - Cycle
By Hazel Dangworth

Catkin - fringed branches strung themselves across the forest path
Warm sunlight latticed shadow - branches on the ground.
High up unseen, birdsong filtered through layers of foliage,
The warp and weft of childhood.

Beyond the super structure of trees, in open sunlight,
Fat catkins swarmed over willows in ditches,
A single butterfly danced ahead,
Sunbathing in pauses on ruts of track.

Returning, the air was cold, silent and sunless,
Illusion's web unravelled,
Only memory left and a long cycle home.

Going To School In Essex
By Helen Reynolds (aged 15)

Braeside School, the school that I attend, is situated in Essex. It is on the border between London and Essex. It is situated across the road from a forest and a large field with a cricket square in the middle. The girls from Bracside can often be seen playing rounder's, running or doing athletics on the field and in the winter we can be seen running through the forest. There are two bus stops close by, which is useful for the people who use the bus to and from school. Outside the school there is a crossing, so it is quite safe to cross the main road outside the school. The school is set back from the road by a semi-circle shaped driveway. The school is quite hidden from the road by large conifer trees. Braeside School is not purpose built, so it is very small and it has some very ornate features that you would not normally expect in a school. The room that is used as the English room for example, has a very decorative border and very old 'drop down' windows that are original. The doors have brass decoration on them under the handle and most, if not all, of the doors in the main building are original and some of them are so heavy because they are so thick, it is hard to move them! There is an original Bell Tower at the back of the school. The school has now been modernised and we have laboratories for our science lessons and even that building has been built to fit in with the style of the main building by using similar bricks. We also have a computer room that will soon have state of the art computers and laptops that we can use in lessons.

I feel that Essex is very different to many other counties because it has such a mix of people from all different backgrounds. There are people who are very privileged and at the same time, there are people who are not so privileged living alongside them. In Essex there is such diversity in all aspects, from schools to the clothes that people wear. Of course, there are the trade mark 'Essex girls' that come from and live in Essex and they are the people that everyone pokes fun at, because of the way they speak using a lot of slang and because of the way that they dress in very short skirts and tight tops. Of course, not everyone is like that. However, Essex is home to a few famous people, Patsy Palmer (Bianca from Eastenders) to name one.

Essex is a good place to go to school in because it is very large, so that means that you meet people from all religions and races and you learn to accept everyone for who they are inside, so in a way you become a better person in my opinion. Overall, I feel that my school is very traditional in the sense of the architecture, but it is very modern in the lessons and facilities aspect. We have computers and laptops, but at the same time, we have grassy wooded grounds to enjoy breaks in. In most schools, the grounds are all tarmac, but in our school grounds we have many listed trees that offer us shade, which means that sometimes when it is really hot we can go out and have our lesson in the gardens. The main lawn is very green and it is kept looking nice by the caretakers and in the summer we have garden furniture out for us to use. Leading up to the grass there are stone steps, yet another clue that the house is Victorian. The steps are quite elaborate with two pillars either side and at the moment, there are flowers on the top of the pillars. Because our school only has around one hundred and fifty students in it, you feel like you know everyone, so Braeside is more like a big extended family than a school. This feeling is good because school does not feel so daunting and it sometimes is very useful that the school is very small when you have to stand up at the front and talk to the school because it is less scary. I can honestly say that if I had the chance to go back in time, to be in Braeside house when the servants' quarters were in use, I definitely would. The servants' quarters are used as cloakrooms now and sometimes I wonder if the narrow cloakroom that I am in used to be a pantry because it is very long and thin. A lot of the rooms have fireplaces that have been boarded up now for insulation purposes, but in some of the rooms you can still see some of the decorative patterns that went around the fireplace. In the garden we have a tennis court that is used for matches. This court doubles up as a netball court. The rooms have an unusual feeling to them because when you look around, there is history all around. On the walls of the English room for example, you can see decorative patterns at the top where the wall meets the ceiling in the shape of a ribbon. I sometimes wonder how many pupils have sat in the seat that I use in classrooms, because the school is quite old. The decor may not have changed much, but the uses of the rooms have. For example, the Maths room as it is now, used to be Miss Wakefield's, the founder of the school's bedroom. The room that is used for photocopying used to be Miss Wakefield's bathroom. All you have to do is use some imagination and you can take yourself back in time and you can imagine yourself in the house as it used to be when it was used as a home in all of its splendour.

I have to say that the best thing about Braeside is the atmosphere. Rather than a school, we are a big family. Every Christmas we have the house Drama and Carol Festival and you do not do things like that in the bigger schools. Although everything else like the lessons that are taught have changed over the years, the general ethos of the school has not changed. I am sure that Miss Wakefield intended the school to be like a family, because she never married herself and it has been said that she saw the students as her family. Because the school is very small, everyone in the school knows everyone's name and most of the time this is good, but at times it can mean that you end up being roped into doing things, like debate for example, because people just put your name down on the list. The house captains know everyone's name and I feel that this gives the impression of being even more like a family and it really proves just how small the school really is. Because you know everyone, you can tell when someone is upset, because you see them at other times and you get to know their character, so it means that you cannot get any peace to sit on your own, because you will get at least one person asking you if you are alright. Because we are a very close knit community more than a school, it means that everyone can get involved in all of the activities that happen, so there is no chance of anyone being left out, which is a good thing for the more quiet people. The people at Braeside are very friendly and I feel that this is because of the community that we are in. Everyone knows what you are like and they grow to respect you for who you are because they grow to know you.

Extracts from other Pupils Essays

The behaviour of the girls in the area is different I'm sure. Blonde hair and short skirts set a bad reputation for girls who look for love in all the wrong places. So much more toned down than the city, but Essex is still a busy place, just not like the chaos that goes on in the streets of the built-up metropolis.
Clare McDonald (aged 14)

Essex is a lovely area, I should know, I live there! I walk to school because I only live down the road from Braeside. I think the area is a friendly area. There are lots of trees, it's peaceful and it's my home.
Isabelle Docker (aged 11)

Braeside is located in Buckhurst Hill, Essex. Buckhurst Hill is a peaceful sub-urban area. In my opinion the people and their lifestyles from around here live up to the stereotypical view Essex is given (Essex girls ect.). Attending school in Essex is something I dislike a lot. It's too materialistic and just has a bunch of posers walking up and down Loughton High Road
Siobhan M. Oliver (aged 14)

On the way to school I see many trees and lots of green, whereas in the big cities there are lots of smoke and cars, not like Essex, where it is peaceful and has many beautiful houses
Mia Bull (aged 14)

I have been here since 1999. It is now 2004 and I have seen big changes in just five years. I can't imagine how different it would seem to a past pupil.
Tessa Kennedy (aged 14)

Braeside school is an all girls' school but it used to be a boys and girls school. I know because of all the school photos that are around the school have boys in the pictures.
Skye Jacobs (aged 11)

Braeside used to have boys in it but the decision was made not to have boys. The thought of not having boys in the school fills some girls with horror and some feel relief. Personally I believe that the environment of Braeside maintains a high standard of learning and education for every-one.
Catherine Waithe-Arnold (aged 14)

I think for my age group it is quite cool being in an all girls' school, although in a couple of years I'll probably wish this was different . Really it's all for the greater good because boys would look really dumb in our school uniform.
Michelle Saltzman (aged 11)

Our school uniform has changed very much. Instead of a brown tunic, it is now a blue tartan skirt, which makes us look very smart and intelligent.
Hayley Docker (aged 14)

I feel that our uniform should be changed because I can't stick wearing a kilt or a skirt. So in winter I think we should have trousers and in the summer either three quarter length trousers or shorts.
Francesca Higgins (aged 11)

When I go to school I feel happy because I am with all my friends but don't feel that happy because I have my lessons. What I really like about Braeside School is that we have lots of holidays but we don't have many teacher training days. I don't like the uniform as much, I don't like the colour.
Manju Minhas (aged 11)

I like going to school in Essex because there are lots of green places with trees and grass. Also there is not a lot of crime in Essex compared to other places.
Zeinab Harding (aged 11)

The Bridge Over The River Roding
At Snakes Lane, Woodford Bridge
By Hazel Dongworth

She recognised the photo at once, the bridge with the three arches, the placid cattle grazing, drinking water. Her son had used this photo fifteen years ago for part of his GCSE coursework on the River Roding. Research had revealed the Roding had often flooded at the lower end of Snakes Lane where the bridge was and in the days before cars, horse and cart took people over to the village, Woodford Bridge, the other side. When flooding made walking impossible, people could get a lift on the horse and cart.

Years later, she and her partner had found a rusty horseshoe in the earth and grass verges by the side of the road, not far from the bridge. They took it home where it now sits on a dresser-shelf, a little bit of local history.

In more recent times, the bridge and the river have been changed to accommodate the building of the M11 motorway, but in the autumn of the year 2000, the Roding flooded again, making the lower end of Snakes Lane impassable, cutting off the Baptist Church, Broadmead Road Flats Sports Ground and Chigwell Road down to Charlie Brown's Roundabout, all built on the river's flood plain. The only building which escaped was the Esso garage, as it's foundations were built at least six feet above the river's banks.

August 2005

End Of The Line
By J Burns

So sad the faces that looked on enviously at swashbuckling
people who had left the train at Mile End, but they were trapped
in the tube to destinations far into the outer suburbs of who-knew-
where,,,
'HAINAULT' ---the end of the line ---could be a place in HOLLAND.
I used to be safe in the streets of Mile End, but life is not like that,
it won't leave you alone, it gnaws at your fibres, tears, patronises,
makes you feel you're not so comfortable in your first floor maisonette
next to the gasworks. The dust chutes blocked up with massive boxes of
Tide washing power, Pledge aerosol cans, modern bugs with old ideas.
So quiet every day like a Sunday, talking quietly.
'Who's that? --- Oh, it's the hydrangeas blowing in the wind'.
Nice gardens, but where are the gardeners? Has the plague struck?
Somebody must have planted them, where are the people?
'Semi-detached Suburbia'
'Do you mind not parking there, it's my space'.
'Sorry!'
'No ball games on the grass!'
'Come in kids ---'
'I wouldn't mind, but the last time I made a pot of tea for new neigh-
bours, they expected it all the time!'
'Who's that knocking? Do I believe in Armageddon, could do with
some excitement.
'Loneliness is the bedmate of the grave'.
Was this really the end of the line,
Or a new beginning?

Photos Of Now And Then
By kind permission of Mr. B Piggot

The Post Office, Barkingside about 1905.
Original Post Office opened in 1863.
Stood where Sainsburys Freezer Centre traded until 1986.
Below: the same view in 1986

Tram Terminus and The Chequers, Barkingside about 1905.
Below: the same view in 1986.

The Chequers, High Street Barkingside, junction with Tanners Lane, about 1900
When this picture was taken the public house was known as the 'Old Chequers
Inn' There is a notice board behind the trees which says "to parlour"
Below: the same view 1988

132

Tanner's Lane, looking towards Barkingside High Street about 1905
Below: the same view 1988

The above photo c1952 shows the site now occupied by Fullwell Cross Library & Swimming baths, High Street, Barkingside. Fullwell Hatch Farm Buildings once stood here. The number 691 trolleybus started service in 1938, it's route was from Barking Broadway via Ilford Lane, Ilford Broadway, Ley Street, Horns Road and with an extension along the High Street, terminating at the "Fairlop Oak" roundabout.

Trolley buses were withdrawn from local service in 1959. Below: A view of the same area, 1987. The Library and Swimming Baths complex was opened in March 1968.

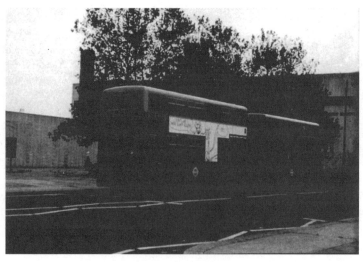

High Street, Barkingside, early 1900's This view shown covers the area at the junction of what is now Waverley Gardens looking towards The Chequers.
The name Barkingside can be traced back to 1538 and was on the extreme edge of the old parish of Barking.
Below: The same view, 1986

Hainault Station, New North Road about 1928
Picture courtesy of British Rail
The station was opened to passengers in 1903. With expectations of trains carrying 1,000 passengers or more, platforms were built over 200yds long. In 1908, with no sign of the expected housing development and with fewer than 20 people using the station each day, the station was closed. It remained closed until 1930 when suburban housing at last reached Hainault. Below: The same view taken in 1987.

Fencepiece Road, Barkingside about 1920.
The origin of the name 'Fencepiece' is uncertain, but the conjecture is that a piece of the forest was 'fenced' in which gave rise to the name. The road existed in 1804. There was also a Fencepiece Farm.
Below: The same view in 1987

Barkingside Station about 1910. Picture courtesy of British Rail.
Opened to passengers in 1903. The station was well placed to serve
Dr Barnardo's Village Homes in Tanners Lane. The homes were often
visited by royalty, who would come by train to Barkingside and this may
be a reason for the ornate style of the building. When Dr Barnardo died in
1905 his body was conveyed by train to the station for burial in the grounds
of the homes. Below: A view of the station taken in 1985.

Cairns Memorial Cottage and Clock Tower, grounds of Dr Barnardo's, Barkingside 1901. The buildings (1887) are named after Earl Cairns, (1819-1885) a former Lord Chancellor and supporter of Dr Barnardo's work. In the background is the Village Church. The original photograph, above, was taken in 1901, by G E Tasker, author of Ilford Past & Present. Below the same view, 1987.

George Newstead's Story

I was born in Wickmere, Norfolk in 1920 and raised in a farm house on a smallholding. Educated in the local village school, I left at 14 to work on a farm carrying out general farm work.

The work horses were the backbone of the farm, their weight and muscle pulled the plough to till the fields and wagons to haul loads. The cutting/binding machine that cut the corn and bundled it up into sheaves was also used to dig up sugarbeet and this machine was the hardest of them all for the horses to pull.

The machine weighed about a ton and it took three horses to pull it around the fields and farmers had to have two or three teams of three horses to enable them to be changed every four hours throughout the day as the heavy work tired them out.

I was 16 when I went to another farm to work, driving a tractor, something that was new to farm work then. This did the work of the horse, ploughing, digging and hauling. One drawback was there was no cover on it so I was exposed to all weathers and conditions.

It was 1939, war had been declared and all the men on farms around had been called up for the Forces. By 1940 I'd had enough of being the only one and although I needn't have gone, as farm work was an occupation essential to the war effort, I was determined to leave.

So on a form I had to complete, I put my job down as Poultry Feeder, which wasn't a reserve occupation. Consequently I was called up. The farmer wasn't very happy at my going, as apart from losing a worker, it was harvest time.

I had to report to the local recruiting office and was interviewed by an officer who asked me what I wanted to do and I promptly replied 'A driver', which was all I wanted to be. 'You don't want to be a driver' he said 'The army is full of them, why not join the Coldstream Guards?'

I couldn't see myself as a Guardsman and politely refused. However, he kept on about this then fortunately left me in the office alone. Then a Sergeant came in and asked what I wanted to do. When I replied 'Driver' he just said ok and put me down as just that. I had to report back later and ended up doing a 6 week driving course at a depot in Stafford.

Later I went with the first army to North Africa, landing in Algiers, then it was off to Bone, then onto Tunis. While in our camp there, troops came down from the front line for a break and one of them asked if we would look after a small dog for them. We said we would and took it off them promising to look after it and it became part of the unit, but unfortunately it was run over by one of our lorry's and killed.

We also had another dog, a Retriever and as we were due to move I was ordered to take it up in the hills and lose it. We tried to get it to jump into a lorry so the order could be carried out, but it refused to get on board and no one would pick it up and put it on. For a while it was safe, but we had to move camp and an Officer ordered us to leave it behind. We couldn't ignore him and in the rush to move on, rather than leave it to suffer, it was decided the best thing to do was to put it down; so one of the men took it away and shot it. Later when we had time to think about it we were quite upset that it had ended like that.

Our move was back to Bone. Our detachment was supposed to be going to Sicily with the 25th Armoured Brigade and their Churchill Tanks. We were to be the runabouts to keep them supplied with spare parts as required, but the posting was cancelled as the terrain in Sicily was considered unsuitable for Churchill's.

Instead, we went to Monte Cassino where the Germans were holding out in the Monastery on the top of the mountain. The Germans were well dug in and it was obvious that terrific battles had taken place there, as the whole of the countryside around the Monte Cassino was one mass of craters caused by the shells and bombs that had been showered down.

We were in a camp away from there and had twenty lorries all placed in a circle back to back and whenever spares had to be carried to the tanks, the lorries would be called out one by one and directed to where the spares could be picked up and where they had to go to.

Later we moved up to what was known as the 'Gothic' line then started to move towards Rome at a rate of about 6-7 miles a day. We ran about all over with spares, but the roads were so full of military traffic, that it was impossible to get around in a straightforward way and for even a simple journey we could be away for two or three day's at a time.

One night in the dark we drove onto a clearing to stop the night and it wasn't until the next day that we found we had parked on an airfield evacuated by the Germans. They had established themselves well there as they had a road lined with all different shops, empty now of course that catered for all their needs.

However, we never realised how lucky we had been as we were told later that the Germans had planted over a hundred booby traps and mines before they left.

As we got nearer to Rome, we were told we could not go into the City as it was being left for the Americans to relieve.

It was April 1945, we had by passed Rome, progressing further North and not being able to get back to the depot. We stopped off in Milan, where I came across a crowd of people on the road.

I was surprised to find that Mussolini and his mistress had been executed by the Partisans and they had hung the pair upside down by the road.

As we advanced further we weren't allowed to settle in Italy and were shipped off to Greece.

The war in Europe ended in May 1945 and I was demobbed in 1946 and went back to Norfolk. There I met a girl who lived in London, a friend of the family and when she returned home, I promised I would get the two o'clock train and meet her at Liverpool Street Station at six. Unfortunately, due to the vagaries of country bus travel, I missed the two o'clock train and never got to London until eight.

The girl was so irate and disagreeable that I walked away from her and while waiting for the next train back to Norfolk, I went into the Railway Buffet and started talking to the girl working behind the counter. That was how I met Stella, my future wife.

I wasn't able to settle down to farm work, as a job that was twenty four hours a day, seven day's a week, seemed too much of a good thing. My main interest now was plumbing. I had been studying and reading all the books I could on the subject, but there didn't seem to be much prospect being a plumber in Norfolk.

I took a job in Romford Gas Works as a pipe fitter, but found I had to clear coke deposited in the Hoppers below ground, right at the bottom of the Retort House.

The end product of turning coal into gas, what was left was a smokeless fuel, coke. After clearing one Hopper after another, I found it was a never ending job as, as fast as they were emptied, they were filled up and decided that was not for me.

1947 was a real hard winter and the gas works sold coke to the public between 8am to midday, Monday to Saturday. Fuel for domestic fires was in short supply and long queues formed outside the works from opening to closing time as people filed through the gate to buy the fuel 'to keep their home fires burning' and keep warm.

A young lad turned up on a Sunday the day the gasworks was closed and pleaded with a worker to let him have some coke as his family were out of fuel and were freezing in the cold.

The worker took pity on him and arranged to throw a bagful over the fence in Crow Lane. However, someone spotted it, reported it and the workman was sacked on the Monday.

I heard they were building prefabricated houses in Straight Road, so went there and said I was a pipe fitter and was taken on to start work on the Monday. So pleased at getting a job, I had to accept it although I realised it would clash with an important day in my life.

It was 1947 and the Saturday before I was due to start work on the Monday, was the day Stella and I married, but not wishing to jeopardise my new job and needing the money, as arranged I went to work on Monday.

We started our new life in Pettits Lane and at that time across the road from us it was all open fields, until in the 1960's six hundred houses were built on the site. I was then earning £6.5s.0d a week. £2 paid the mortgage, £4 for household and the 5s saw me through the week.

Many prefabricated houses were being erected in Straight Road, as they were all over London. Our job (four of us on this site) was to put in all the pipe work to provide the services, then after laying it out as necessary, with pipe ends left above what would be the floor level, concrete was poured over to form the foundation slab to build on. Then it was a simple job as the houses were erected to connect up to provide water, sewage, gas and electricity.

The prefabs came from Southampton and four lorry loads equalled a complete house. They were delivered on a Friday, a gang of men would turn up and on Monday there was another new home. A lorry turned up one day and I was surprised to see the driver was a man I'd been in the army with.

To further my plumbing knowledge and to pursue the trade further, I signed on for a years plumbing course at Longbridge Technical College an excellent theoretical and practical course, it improved my plumbing skills no end.

It was 1948 and I heard men were wanted at a new estate being built in Hainault. I had an interview and was taken on as a plumber by a firm Denton Hellyer. Starting on the houses being built at the Grange Hill end of Manford Way, we worked our way down towards the rents office. It took about four days to do all the plumbing in a house and for most it was a butlers sink in the kitchen with a tap fitted to the wall with three screws, but a bathroom was installed.

A number of houses built were called 'Finer Houses'. Shuttering would be erected in the shape of the house walls, with window spaces blocked out, graded clinker would be delivered from the gasworks, mixed up with cement then poured into the shuttering and left to set. One of the snags was that the mix never usually got in under the window spaces and had to be filled in separately when the shuttering came down.

French was the main contractor on the site and hundreds of men were employed. I used to bike to work, but double deck buses were used to fetch others in the morning and take them home at night.

French also had accommodation huts on a field off Barley Lane to house men who didn't live locally; also had a large canteen providing food and refreshments for the workmen and it was located in Manford Way where the Community Centre now stands.

To provide refreshments at tea breaks, a van travelled round at 10am and 3pm serving up a cup of tea for threehapence and buns at tuppence (about one and a half new pence).

Gangs of men went around with chestnut paling fences to fix the boundaries of gardens and the first school on the estate was completed in Manford Way. I went on to do the plumbing on houses in New North Road and Elmbridge Road.

There was some excitement on the site when the hut that was the Office for the Architects caught fire and burned to the ground with all the plans, papers and documents they had for the job in hand. No doubt duplicates were soon made available to keep things going.

There were strikes on the site called by the Union official that affected all workers. They were off for a week over bonuses. Another week was lost in a dispute with Management over the provision of soap and towels for the men to clean up before they left work.

Then the Union Official involved was sacked by the Management and the men were called out in sympathy to get him re-instated. They were out for another week and he was taken back on, but shortly after packed the job in and left the site.

After two years at Hainault, I moved on to a housing estate being built at Avely, later moving on to Harold Hill, another new estate. There I was working with six other men erecting slab housing and doing the pipe work.

My next job took me to another housing estate at Waltham Abbey where I stayed for two years, before going onto the Bank of England Printing Works in 1961 where I spent one of the coldest winters I can remember.

By now, I was a Member of the Institute of Plumbers and a Registered Corgi Gas Engineer. I left the Printing Works and started my own business that progressed very well, getting plenty of work in the area that kept myself and the men I employed really busy until I retired in 1985.

20.02.06

The Forest Sleeps
By Lewis Button

The forest sleeps no soul is heard
Not even lonely singing bird.
No star shining through the trees
Please listen, no buzzing of the bees.
No flapping sound of birds a' winging,
No nightingale or blackbird singing.

Just one who gives his t'witt t'woo
That wise old owl is passing through
A sudden swoop his wings a' flapping
He pounces on a mouse caught a' napping.
A cunning fox with, raucous voice
Struts his stuff the vixens choice.

If you just listen so very still
You might just catch the nightjar's trill.
Try not to let me catch you yawning.
Soon it will be daylight dawning.
You'll see that dog fox mouth full of feathers.
Takes his spoils home, in all weathers.

That's Hainault Forest after dark.
No peaceful stroll in the park.
All life is there in every part my dear
A circle of life no faint hearts you'll find here
The sun comes up a different story
All nature stands with majestic glory.